Pound

Open Guides to Literature

Series Editor: Graham Martin (Professor of Literature, The Open University)

Current titles

Graham Holderness: *Wuthering Heights*
P.N. Furbank: Pound
Graham Martin: *Great Expectations*
Roderick Watson: MacDiarmid

Titles in preparation include

Angus Calder: Byron
David Pirie: Shelley
Walford Davies: Dylan Thomas
Roger Day: Larkin
Jeanette King: *Jane Eyre*
Dennis Walder: Hughes

Ezra Pound (Camera Press. Photograph: Horsle Tappe)

P.N. FURBANK

Pound

Open University Press
Milton Keynes · Philadelphia

Open University Press
Open University Educational Enterprises Limited
12 Cofferidge Close
Stony Stratford
Milton Keynes MK11 1BY, England

and
242 Cherry Street
Philadelphia, PA 19106, USA

First published 1985

British Library Cataloguing in Publication Data

Furbank, P.N.
  Pound.—(Open guides to literature)
  1. Pound, Ezra—Criticism and interpretation
  I. Title   II. Series
  811'.52   PS3531.082Z/
  ISBN 0–335–15088–8
  ISBN 0–335–15079–9 Pbk

Library of Congress Cataloging in Publication Data

Main entry under title:
Furbank, Philip Nicholas.
  Pound.

  (Open guides to literature)
  Bibliography: p.
  Includes index.
  1. Pound, Ezra, 1885–1972—Criticism and interpretation.
I. Title. II. Series.
PS3531.082Z634   1985   811'.52   85–5123
ISBN 0–335–15088–8
ISBN 0–335–15079–9 (pbk.)

Text design by Clarke Williams
Typeset by Cambrian Typesetters, Frimley, Surrey
Printed in Great Britain by J.W. Arrowsmith, Bristol

Contents

Series Editor's Preface

The intention of this series is to provide short introductory books about major writers, texts, and literary concepts for students of courses in Higher Education which substantially or wholly involve the study of Literature.

The series adopts a pedagogic approach and style similar to that of Open University material for Literature courses. *Open Guides* aim to inculcate the reading 'skills' which many introductory book in the field tend, mistakenly, to assume that the reader already possesses. They are, in this sense, 'teacherly' texts, planned and written in a manner which will develop in the reader the confidence to undertake further independent study of the topic. They are 'open' in two senses. First, they offer a three-way tutorial exchange between the writer of the *Guide*, the text or texts in question, and the reader. They invite reades to join in an exploratory discussion of texts, concentrating on their key aspects and on the main problems which readers, coming to the texts for the first time, are likely to encounter. The flow of a *Guide* 'discourse' is established by putting questions for the reader to follow up in a tentative and searching spirit, guided by the writer's comments, but not dominated by an over-arching and single-mindedly-pursued argument or evaluation, which itself requires to be 'read'.

Guides are also 'open' in a second sense. They assume that literary texts are 'plural', that there is no end to interpretation, and that it is for the reader to undertake the pleasurable task of discovering meaning and value in such texts. *Guides* seek to provide, in compact form, such relevant biographical, historical and cultural information as bears upon the reading of the text, and they point the reader to a selection of the best available critical discussions of it. They are not in themselves concerned to propose, or to counter, particular readings of the texts, but rather to put *Guide* readers in a position to do that for themselves. Experienced travellers learn to dispense with guides, and so it should be for readers of this series.

This *Open Guide* to the poetry of Ezra Pound is best used in conjunction with his *Selected Poems, 1908–1959* (Faber, 1975). Page references in the *Guide* are to this edition.

Graham Martin

Acknowledgements

Grateful acknowledgement is made to Faber and Faber Ltd for the reprint by permission of poems from *Collected Shorter Poems* by Ezra Pound, and to New Directions for the reprint by permission of the same poems from *Personae* (copyright 1926 by Ezra Pound). Grateful acknowledgement is also made to Constable and Co. and Alfred A. Knopf Inc. for Arthur Waley's translation 'Green, green, The grass by the river bank' in *170 Chinese poems* and in *Translations from the Chinese*.

My thanks go to the Open University for permission to develop this book from material originally contributed to their Twentieth Century Poetry Course.

1. Ezra Pound and 'Modernism'

There was a major revolution in English verse just before the 1914–18 war, in which the American poet Ezra Pound played a leading part, and which is now generally called by the name of 'modernism'. It is a name to be used with caution, as it can be rather misleading. In the first place, it was not used at the time, but was coined much later by scholars. Ezra Pound did not call himself a 'modernist'; he called himself an 'Imagist', and later, for a time, a 'Vorticist'. As for T.S. Eliot, he did not call himself by the name of any new movement; though later on, to the amazement of some of his followers, he declared himself a classicist in literature, a royalist in politics and an Anglo-Catholic in religion. Secondly, 'modernist' does not mean the same as 'modern'. The implication of the word, as I shall use it here, is that the movement is now over and may be seen as part of history. Thirdly, the name, of course, does not apply only to poetry. If we are to use the term at all, we must bear in mind that there was 'modernism' in prose fiction, and in music, and in painting, sculpture and architecture. If Pound and Eliot were 'modernists', then so, certainly, were Stravinsky and Schönberg, Picasso and Brancusi. Some scholars speak of 'modernism' in philosophy, theology and psychology, and even in mathematics and physics. And here we come up against a danger in the word. It is too convenient, you can always fall back on it when you do not mean anything in particular.

What is indisputably true is that there was an extraordinary outburst of intellectual and artistic activity in the early 1900s. It

was one of the great periods in Western culture, and further, it was
an age of discovery. Everywhere the emphasis was on the *new*. Ezra
Pound entitled a volume of his essays *Make It New*, and it might
have been the slogan for the age. New movements, new trends,
followed one another with bewildering rapidity. The whole
foundations of thought and knowledge seemed to be – and indeed
were – shifting. One can make other simple generalizations. One
can say that culture in this period was peculiarly cosmopolitan:
Paris was aware of Vienna, and Vienna of St Petersburg, in a way
that has not been true in many periods in history. It was also
peculiarly eclectic. Artists felt themselves the inheritors of all past
ages and of all parts of the globe, and free to make use of them and
pillage them as they wished. Stravinsky flirted with Russian folk
music, with Viennese eighteenth-century music, with Bach and with
African tribal music. Ezra Pound donned the mask of a Provençal
troubadour, a Latin poet of the Empire, and a classical Chinese
lyricist.

It does not follow from all this, though, that what was
occurring was one movement – that there was something called
'modernism' trying to break out, like dry rot, all over the place.
That is to give the word too definite a meaning; we would do better
to go to the other extreme and define 'modernism' simply as 'all the
new thought developing round about 1900–10'.

I think, though, there was more to it than that. For one thing,
'modernist' artists and thinkers were intensely aware of one
another's work. Painters, in particular, sometimes collaborated
very closely; it has been said, I do not know how truly, that Picasso
and Braque, who invented Cubism in 1908 or thereabouts,
sometimes could hardly remember later which of them had painted
a particular canvas. Likewise, it often happened that a painter
would try to achieve in painting the same thing as a poet whom he
admired, and vice versa. I choose these as clear and specific
examples of interrelations between 'modernists'. Beyond them
spreads out a web of innumerable links, influences and cross-
currents, both conscious and unconscious, between the artists and
thinkers of the time, and we shall follow certain threads of this web
in the present book.

This still does not mean that there was something called
'modernism', if one means by that a definite movement with a
definite set of doctrines. And for this reason I shall not, myself,
offer a definition of 'modernism', for I think that more would be
lost than gained by it. Let us think a little further about what sort of
term 'modernism' is. It is not a term like 'Marxism' or 'Impres-

sionism', which can be quite easily defined. It is not even a term like 'Conservatism'. For, though there are many conflicting definitions of Conservatism, there must come a moment, if you use the word at all, when you have to define it. A Tory candidate would look very foolish if he said he was sorry, but he couldn't quite define Conservatism, 'though of course he knew what it was'. A term that resembles 'modernism' more closely, I suggest, is 'the Renaissance'. Everyone defines the Renaissance differently; they even date it differently, by as much as a century. Nevertheless, it is a useful term, and means somewhat more than just 'Leonardo da Vinci, the Medici, Shakespeare and Machiavelli'.

Coming then to English poetry: which were the first poems in English to which we might apply the term 'modernist'? My list would be as follows: certain poems written in 1908 and thereafter by what came to be known as the Imagist school of poets; various early poems by T.S. Eliot, especially 'The Love Song of J. Alfred Prufrock', written in 1910–11 and first published in a periodical in 1915; D.H. Lawrence's sequence of free verse poems, *Look! We Have Come Through!*, published in 1917. And – since the midwife of 'modernism' in English verse was Ezra Pound – it seems right to include the two volumes, by no means his first, in which he attained maturity as a poet: I mean *Cathay (1915)* and *Homage to Sextus Propertius (1917)*.

Viewing it in this way, we have a movement that began some six years before the First World War and which does not appear to have been greatly deflected by the war. But also a movement that came rather late in Britain. Much had been happening already in literature in Paris and Vienna; and indeed important things had been happening in Britain, if one thinks of prose fiction. By 1908 Joyce had made, or was making, profound innovations in fictional technique. Prose fiction was in advance of poetry generally in Britain at this time: Henry James and Conrad had reflected more deeply on their art and made stricter artistic rules for themselves than any contemporary poets. And it became a favourite theme of Ezra Pound's that poets needed to learn from the prose writers – above all from Flaubert.

In regard to English literature, there is an important point to remember. As the British Empire expanded in the century's closing years, so, culturally speaking, did Britain withdraw from Europe. 'In the last decade of Victoria's reign', says Samuel Hynes[1], 'one could not buy a translation of Zola's *La Terre*, or Dostoevsky's *The Idiot* or *The Brothers Karamasov* in London, or see a public performance of Ibsen's *Ghosts*, or look at any pictures by a French

Impressionist in any gallery, either public or private. The new thought of Europe had been kept out of England, as though by quarantine.' Thus, a prime need of British writers in the early 1900s, if they took their art seriously, was simply to educate themselves, to catch up with developments of twenty years earlier in France and other European countries. Joyce conducted such a self-education, round about the turn of the century, thereby becoming more than a home-grown Irish writer. Eliot did so too, and his reading of Arthur Symons's *The Symbolist Movement in Literature* (1899) round about 1908 was a turning point in his development. And Ezra Pound becomes significant here. Pound, a tireless though wildly unsystematic self-educator, had also a passion for educating others. (Gertrude Stein, the American *avant-garde* novelist, called Pound a 'village explainer' – adding that, not being a village, she did not feel the need of him.[2]) One of Pound's enterprises was to take Yeats in hand, at the elder poet's invitation, in order that he might 'modernize' him.

Another need of the writer and artist was to fortify his independence. Given the stagnant condition of official English culture, and the spread of cheap fiction and mass circulation dailies, writers with high ambitions could hardly hope to be popular, as their predecessors had been. They might, to begin with at least, have to write mainly for fellow writers, a tiny audience indeed; and to face this fact and not let it daunt them called for much toughness. The writers of the English 1890s had faced it in their own way, a tragic way. They made a tragic drama of their relations with the public, resorting to absinthe or 'diabolism' or taking refuge in Catholicism (though perhaps 'taking refuge' is not a fair way of putting it). Living out their poetry in their lives, in this way, they quickly burned themselves out, ending up in alcoholic wards or as suicides. There may have been integrity in this, but in the long run it was bad for poetry, for poetry requires a back-breaking labour. We may recall Yeats's lines in 'Adam's Curse':

> . . . A line will take us hours maybe;
> Yet if it does not seem a moment's thought,
> Our stitching and unstitching has been naught.
> Better go down upon your marrow-bones
> And scrub a kitchen pavement, or break stones
> Like an old pauper, in all kinds of weather;
> For to articulate sweet sounds together
> Is to work harder than all these, and yet
> Be thought an idler by the noisy set
> Of bankers, schoolmasters, and clergymen
> The martyrs call the world.[3]

Thus, a poet needs to keep in physical training, and to husband his resources.

The *avant-garde* writers and artists of the new century took the lesson, and what we see in them is the development of a tougher, more resilient, more cheerful and intransigent attitude towards society. What they wanted, above all, was to *work*, to be allowed to produce – and by hook or by crook they set themselves to secure the minimum conditions for this. They presented themselves to the world, and to themselves, as artificers, with tools and equipment kept in good working order. They cultivated not a suffering but a buoyant attitude towards society – teasing it, or bullying it, according to their temperament. I am generalizing wildly, again, but this is not an altogether false picture of the public stance of Joyce and Eliot, as of Picasso and Stravinsky and many others of the *avant-garde* of the time.

Now, Ezra Pound, when he appeared on the London scene in 1908, was a supreme example of this attitude. He was tirelessly energetic, indefatigably creative, a *poseur* and a pest, but someone who prized, above all, what he called 'factive intelligence',[4] the determination to *make* things. In a way, his art and his propaganda were one; he hammered at the stupidity of the British reading public with the same energy, if not the same precision, as he 'hammered' at poems or as a sculptor might hammer at marble. However, to believe, as he did, that art should be nothing but art, should contain no extraneous ingredients, is not the same thing as to believe in 'art for art's sake'. On the contrary, Pound came to believe strongly in the social value of art. He considered that artists braced and purified society by their example – by exhibiting self-discipline and by eschewing flabbiness, sentimentality and sloppiness of mind. Poets, in particular, had a social function, in his view, since they deal with words, which are the natural bond of society. Thus, their duty was to defend the language and keep it in good order.

The degree of Pound's influence on British poetry in the period round about the First World War is a matter of debate. There are those who say that it had been exaggerated and that, for instance, Yeats and Eliot would have developed much in the way that they did had Pound never existed – that he was useful to them less as a teacher than as a propagandist and because he confirmed them in decisions already taken. There may be something in this. But perhaps that is what 'influence' often is: a confirmation, a support and encouragement, rather than a cancelling of what one has done hitherto. Writers and artists are influenced most fruitfully when

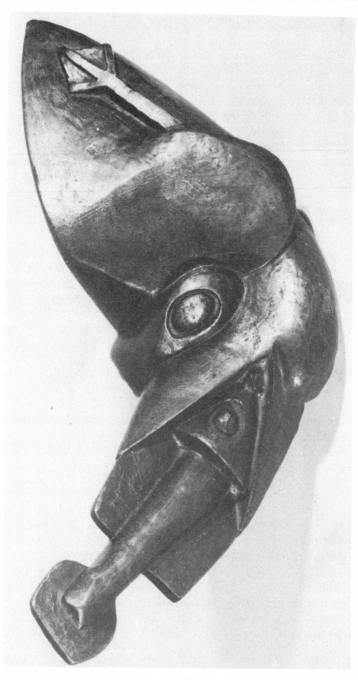

Bird swallowing a fish (c. 1914) by Henri Gaudier — Brzeska (Tate Gallery)

they *choose* to be influenced. And on the other hand both Yeats and Eliot certainly said that they had been influenced by Pound 'He . . . helps me to get back to the definite and concrete and away from abstractions', said Yeats. To talk over a poem with him was like getting his friend Lady Gregory to put a sentence into dialect. 'All becomes clear and natural.'[5] Again, here is what Eliot said, in a review of Pound's *Collected Poems* in *The Dial*, 1928:

> He [Pound] has enabled a few persons, including myself, to improve their verse sense; so that he has improved poetry through other men as well as by himself. I cannot think of anyone writing verse, of our generation and the next, whose verse (if any good) has not been improved by the study of Pound's. . . A man who devises new rhythms is a man who extends and refines our sensibility; and that is not merely a matter of 'technique'. I have, in recent years, cursed Mr Pound often enough; for I am never sure that I can call my verse my own; just when I am most pleased with myself, I find that I have caught up some echo from a verse of Pound's.[6]

Perhaps the most remarkable example of all of Pound's influence on fellow-poets is the fact that Eliot's *The Waste Land* (1922) owes its present form, to a very considerable degree, to Ezra Pound, who edited it at Eliot's request, suggesting quite ruthless alterations and curtailments. (You can see the evidence in a facsimile of the manuscript, with his annotations, published by Valerie Eliot in 1974.)[7]

Let me give a few facts about Pound's life. He was born in 1885 in the frontier town of Hailey, Idaho, where his grandfather (reputed to come from a family of horse thieves) had become a prosperous citizen. When Pound was three years old, the family moved to Philadelphia, his father taking a post there in the United States Mint, and it was here that Pound spent his childhood and schooldays. At the age of fifteen he decided to be a poet and began to write verse. He also resolved at this time that by the age of thirty he would know more about poetry than any man living; and during the six years of his university education he did his best to realize this ambition, reading omnivorously in English, Latin and the Romance literatures. He had originally planned an academic career, but his first and only teaching post, at Wabash College, in Crawfordsville, Indiana, came to an abrupt close as the result of a scandal (Pound, it appears, having shocked local opinion by giving his bed to a young travelling actress). Unregretfully, he set off for Venice, where he studied the art of the Renaissance and published a volume of poems, *A Lume Spento*. From there, with three pounds sterling in his pocket, he moved on, in this same year 1908, to London, where

Ezra Pound by Wyndham Lewis (Tate Gallery)

he quickly found his way into literary circles, meanwhile scratching a living by polytechnic lecturing. At this time he was very much the flamboyant, Swinburnian 'poet', growing his hair long, and wearing jade earrings and shoes of different colours. Before long, he had achieved a wide influence over the *avant-garde* English literary scene. Part of his original intention in coming to Europe had been to meet Yeats; this occurred in 1910, and a year or two later he for a time became a sort of secretary to Yeats.

For a moment just before the 1914–18 war he conceived grandiose ideas of a total renaissance of the arts, with London as its headquarters. The war disrupted these plans; and in 1921, Pound, who felt a growing dislike of British culture and what he thought its hostility to serious art, abandoned London for Paris, moving on from there to Italy in 1924. He was by now an adherent of Major C.H. Douglas's Social Credit theories, which confirmed his conviction that the decay of the arts, together with wars, unemployment and all the other ills of the West, were due to the toleration of 'usury'. He was using the medieval name of this sin as shorthand for the capitalist system. By now he had moved away very far from an 'Art for Art's Sake' standpoint and was intensely political, becoming virulently anti-Semitic and an admirer of Mussolini, whom he regarded as the statesman most nearly resembling an artist. (He thought of Mussolini as an 'artificer', and 'the Debunker *par excellence*'.) He settled in Italy in the mid-1920s, and during the Second World War he broadcast on behalf of the Fascists,[8] and in 1945 he was captured by the American Army and imprisoned for three weeks in an open air 'cage' near Pisa. As a traitor he was in danger of the death penalty, but his lawyers managed to have him declared insane, and he spent the next thirteen years in St Elizabeth's mental hospital near Washington – being released eventually in 1958 without having to face trial.

Pound's career stirs admiration, horror and pity. His committal to St Elizabeth's was mainly a device to save his life; but, if not mad, he seems to have been far gone in delusion on certain subjects during the 1930s. (He made a lightning visit to America in 1939, believing that if he could speak with the President he might prevent the war.) All the more striking and moving is it, therefore, that in that prison cage near Pisa, at the nadir of his fortunes, he retrieved the balance of his mind and conceived the *Pisan Cantos*, which have a claim to be thought his finest achievement.

In St Elizabeth's he wrote and corresponded voluminously, and on his release he continued for a few years to add to *The Cantos*, falling thereafter into silence, both as a writer and as a man. His few utterances during his last years (he died in November 1972) suggested that his silence was, in part, an act of contrition.

Pound devoted almost all the later part of his poetic career to a single work, his vast and hugely ambitious epic poem, *The Cantos*, a work which almost no one regards as a complete success. He did not regard it so himself and in old age murmured about having 'botched' it.[9] *The Cantos* were to have been the *Odyssey* or *Iliad* or *Divine Comedy* of their age, a celebration of the whole 'mind of Europe'; and even Pound's warmest admirers would not grant it quite that status. The word 'failure' hangs over the poem; but if a failure, how disastrous, how complete? Even today, few critics have made up their minds upon this question. The scheme of the poem, if it has a scheme, still eludes them, and this raises the issue of what a 'scheme' in the case of a modern long poem can be. On the other hand even its denigrators (and it has some fierce ones) admit the poem possesses passages of extraordinary beauty and originality; and can a work that contains such achievements be called a 'failure'?

By the time he began *The Cantos* in the form that we know them, Pound was already a mature poet who had found his direction and knew what he wanted to say in poetry. One may name the years 1914–19 as the ones in which he came to maturity. He had begun *The Cantos* somewhere about 1915 but ran into difficulties, and eventually, in 1922 or thereabouts, he made a fresh start. By that time he had published three other major works which, together with certain fine and original shorter poems, will always be enough to give him a reputation. The major works I am thinking of are *Cathay* (1915). *Homage to Sextus Propertius* (1919) and *Hugh Selwyn Mauberley* (1920). They are works very different from one another, and together they exhibit many of the themes and technical innovations on which *The Cantos* were built. It is these three works I shall concentrate on especially in this *Guide*.

Before this, however, I must give some account of the early Pound; and it will be convenient to begin, though a little out of chronological sequence, with his 'Imagist' period, since it was through this that he first exercised a reforming infuence on the English literary scene.

2. Imagism

The Imagist movement, of which Pound became the theorist and leading spokesman, may be said to have had its birth in a dining-club founded in London in 1909 by the poet and philosopher T.E. Hulme and another (now rather forgotten) poet, F.S. Flint. Hulme was a powerful and original thinker on philosophy and aesthetics, standing for a new tough-minded brand of classicism – anti-Romantic, anti-humanistic and, in its emphasis on 'discipline', perhaps with hindsight to be described as potentially proto-fascist. He and Flint, who was an expert on French *Symboliste* poetry, evolved a literary doctrine the prime tenet of which was the need for 'absolutely accurate presentation and no verbiage',[1] and at about this time Hulme produced a handful of admirable brief poems in the spirit of this doctrine.

Ezra Pound, a friend of Hulme's, although their relationship was a trifle edgy, was invited to join the dining-club and soon displayed an intention of taking the new movement over – in which, since Hulme's interests were not really centred on poetry, he eventually succeeded. Round about 1912 he found a name ('Imagism') for the kind of verse that Hulme and Flint had sponsored, and two recruits were attracted to the movement, Richard Aldington and the American poet 'H.D.' (Hilda Doolittle) whom Aldington was shortly to marry. Showing much generous enthusiasm on their behalf, he managed to place poems by them in the magazine *Poetry*, recently founded by Harriet Monroe, and in the pages of the same magazine published a statement of Imagist principles entitled 'A Few Don'ts'.[2] He also appended to his own collection of verse *Ripostes* (1912) five poems by Hulme, jokingly entitling them Hulme's 'Complete Poetical Works'. In 1914 he edited anonymously an anthology, *Des Imagistes*, which included poems by H.D., Flint, Amy Lowell, William Carlos Williams, James Joyce and Ford Madox Ford. At this point, however, he found his

hold over the movement challenged by the energetic American poet
and publicist Amy Lowell, who appeared in London in the summer
of 1914, organized and paid for an Imagist dinner and made
arrangements with a group of poets to produce a series of annual
Imagist anthologies. (It duly appeared as *Some Imagist Poets* in
1915, 1916 and 1917.) This was the signal for Pound, who felt
himself out-manoeuvred, to bow out. He was anyway beginning to
feel Imagism too constricting a doctrine, and he proceeded to throw
his energies into a new movement, called 'Vorticism', which I shall
discuss later.[3]

    As has been seen, the prime tenet of the Imagist movement was
a demand for 'absolutely accurate presentation and no verbiage'.
Let us test a poem by Ezra Pound according to this criterion,

Fan-Piece, for Her Imperial Lord

O fan of white silk,
clear as frost on the grass-blade,
You also are laid aside.

Is this a poem at all, we might ask; What does it say? What is it
about? Is it a description and, if so, to what point? I will do my best
to answer these questions. If the poem evokes any feeling in you at
all at a first reading, it may be nothing more precise than 'fragility'
or 'delicacy'; but if it does as much as this, I would like you to
ponder on how it comes to do so. What is there to cling to? Well,
first, I think, a contrast between the inanimate and the living: the
white of the silk fan is plainly such a fresh, 'living' white that this
inanimate thing puts one in mind of living and evanescent things,
like frost and grass. But, next, if the poem itself seems so fragile, so
insubstantial, could there not be a simple reason for this – that
Pound wants it to *resemble* a delicate Chinese fan? We remember
that a classical Chinese poem might actually be written on silk, in
exquisite calligraphy, so that a poem and a fan would not be such
very diverse things. But then, what is one to make of that last line,
'You also are laid aside' – for the whole poem, such as it is, seems to
lead up to this line. What does it mean? The thing to do, in a case
like this, is to let the line lie in one's mind, without trying to *force* a
meaning from it, till suggestions and implications dawn.

    Certain things are clear: the woman speaking has a fellow
feeling for her fan. This inanimate object symbolizes for her
something evanescent in her own life, which has to be renounced or
resigned. But what that is, we may not be able to guess with
certainty; though it will be something that a fan *would*, naturally,

symbolize – something to do with the life of a high-born lady or fashionable courtesan. My own first guess at the sense was that a bride has to give up modesty (hiding her face with a fan); in making, or painting, a fan for her husband, or 'Imperial Lord', she is, as it were, making him a present of her modesty or virginity. This makes a beautiful poem, I think, but, as it turns out, not the right one! For I find that the poem, or at least the Chinese original, is about a discarded mistress, who is to be 'laid aside' or 'put on the shelf' by her 'lord' or noble lover (so she will no longer have occasion to ply her fan or exercise her attractions). I do not intend to feel too ashamed of my error, for I had enjoyed and loved the poem for years before I ever got down to working out the meaning of that last line, and the discovery does not fundamentally change the poem for me. (though I think it does improve it). The lesson, perhaps, is how much of the real meaning of a poem of this kind lies as much in its *shape* as in its content. Every detail of its shape counts, and this is the justification of the doctrine: 'no verbiage'. This poem, especially in the way it culminates in that last line, resembles more than anything a gesture, a gesture performed with consummate grace – I might add, a gesture like the handling of a fan.

It was Pound who christened the movement with the name 'Imagism', and sometime in 1912 he and his fellow poets 'H.D.' (Hilda Doolittle) and Richard Aldington formulated three principles of *Imagism*:

1   Direct treatment of the 'thing', whether subjective or objective.
2   To use absolutely no word that does not contribute to the presentation.
3   As regarding rhythm: to compose in the sequence of the musical phrase, not in sequence of a metronome.

Pound also gave his definition of an 'Image':

An 'Image' is that which presents an intellectual and emotional complex in an instant of time. . .It is the presentation of such a 'complex' instantaneously which gives that sense of sudden liberation; that sense of freedom from time limits and space limits; that sense of sudden growth, which we experience in the presence of the greatest works of art.[4]

As you will see, Pound lays stress on the instantaneity of the 'Image'; it 'is that which presents an intellectual and emotional complex *in an instant of time*'. What this reveals is that Pound wants poetry to approach closer to (painting) and (sculpture)

Literature is a time-bound art; you have to read the beginning before the middle, and the middle before the end; it is a matter of one thing after another. Painting and sculpture, on the other hand, are not time- or succession-bound. You can begin by looking at a painting or a sculpture where you like; and in a sense, it is possible to take in a painting or a sculpture at a single glance. Pound was deeply impressed by Post-Impressionist painting and modern sculpture, and part of his motive in demanding 'use absolutely no word that does not contribute to the presentation' was a yearning to rival the plastic arts.

We are brought back to a general characteristic of 'modernism' in the arts. One of its tenets was that art should be nothing but art; that is to say, it should not compromise with entertainment, or instruction, or any other purpose extraneous to art. Even Impressionist painting, though considered in its time as very iconoclastic, does not pass the 'modernist' test; for it continued to give the spectator various enjoyments which, in a strict view, were not intrinsic to art. An Impressionist landscape, for instance, gave something of the same experience as would be received from walking in the countryside. This seemed to the 'modernist' a kind of impurity: a painting or a poem need not be a copy of anything in nature. Natural objects and art objects were different and equal, and the artist was not the slave, but the rival, of nature or God.

We must now consider how this theory applies to poetry. At first there might seem to be a contradiction between asserting that a poem should not be a 'copy' of anything in nature, and the demand for 'direct treatment of the "thing" ', as prescribed by the Imagists. It is not really so, however. To begin with, Imagist poems work by comparing one thing with another, giving equal value to each. Consider Pound's poem 'A Song of the Degrees' (*Selected Poems*, p. 48). It is an elusive poem, which seems to be implying some ethical issue involved in an artist's choice of colours. Chinese colours (in silk-paintings or porcelain) have a natural 'honesty', which coloured Venetian-style glass, with its refraction and its shimmering and 'shot' effects, lacks. Such an imputed relationship between an artist's choice of materials and large ethical and even political issues becomes an important theme later in Pound's *Cantos*, especially the 'Usura' Cantos 45 and 51. However, I bring the poem in here because of the lines:

The wind moves above the wheat —
With a silver crashing,
A thin war of metal.

These lines register, very precisely, a perception about landscape –
the movement of wheat-stalks in a summer wind, their collision
heard as a tiny 'crashing'. But so much emphasis is thrown on the
term of comparison, silver (the clashing of silver objects), and this
evocation of metal is pursued so insistently in the following lines,
about the sun and the melting of its 'golden disc', that you could
almost read the lines as being *about* metals, rather than about
landscape: i.e. it is not quite clear which is 'tenor' (the thing
presented) and which is 'vehicle' (the thing to which it is
compared). One would never be tempted to speak of such a poem
as a 'copy' of anything in nature, with the pejorative implication (a
'mere copy', i.e. something second-hand) that the word carries.

Another respect in which Imagist verse differs from traditional
verse is in regard to *statement*. If you think of almost any poem by,
say, Wordsworth or Tennyson or Thomas Hardy, you will see that
it is making some statement, some direct comment on life. To take
an example at random: Thomas Hardy's 'The Oxen' says (I am
paraphrasing brutally) that, though modern man cannot literally
believe the country superstition that at midnight on Christmas Eve
the cattle go down on their knees, nevertheless he may still
poignantly wish to believe it. Now let us take a famous two-line
Imagist poem of Pound's, 'In a Station of the Metro':

> The apparition of these faces in the crowd;
> Petals on a wet, black bough.
>
> *(Selected Poems*, p. 53)

However hard you look at this poem, you will find it impossible to
squeeze any such statement about life out of it. The poet is saying:
'Here is a perception or observation about the external world: I
leave you to piece out its human meaning'. Pound gave a very
instructive account of how this poem came to be written:

> Three years ago in Paris I got out of a 'metro' train at La Concorde,
> and saw suddenly a beautiful face, and then another and another,
> and then a beautiful child's face, and then another beautiful woman,
> and I tried all day to find words for what this had meant to me, and I
> could not find any words that seemed to me worthy, or as lovely as
> that sudden emotion. And that evening, as I went home along Rue
> Raynouard, I was still trying and I found, suddenly, the expression. I
> do not mean that I found words, but there came an equation. . .not
> in speech, but in little splotches of colour. . .That is to say, my
> experience in Paris should have gone into paint. If instead of colour I
> had perceived sound or planes in relation, I should have expressed it
> in music or in sculpture. Colour was, in that instance, the 'primary
> pigment': I mean that it was the first adequate equation that came
> into consciousness.

. . .The 'one image poem' is a form of superposition, that is to say, it is one idea set on top of another. I found it useful in getting out of the impasse in which I had been left by my metro emotion. I wrote a thirty-line poem, and destroyed it because it was what we call work 'of second intensity'. Six months later I made a poem half that length; a year later I made the following *hokku*-like sentence:

The apparition of these faces in the crowd;
Petals on a wet, black bough.

. . .In a poem of this sort one is trying to record the precise instant when a thing outward and objective transforms itself, or darts into a thing inward and subjective.[5]

I think it would be legitimate to guess that the abortive versions that Pound mentions came nearer to making a 'statement' and that it was this 'statement' element that he eventually eliminated. This is not to say, however – or so I understand Pound's view – that such a poem does not have a human meaning. He believed in a 'human nature' – or, in his own words, 'a sort of permanent basis in humanity' (see p.19) – and in poems as being addressed to it. A poem is an intuition about life; and if it is successful, if the perception is rendered accurately, the reader, by re-enacting the perception, will be enabled to share the intuition. (The theory, I should mention, is one that has more recently been under attack from Structuralist and Post-structuralist critics, who tend to deny the reality of a permanent 'human nature' and to regard the reader's activity as something other than a mere re-enactment of the author's intuition.)

Let us approach Imagism, finally, in another and easier way. Imagism is not merely a theory or a movement; it is also, for each of the Imagist poets, a style. One can recognize Pound's 'Imagist' style quite easily. Consider these two poems of his:

April

Nympharum membra disjecta[6]
Three spirits came to me
And drew me apart
To where the olive boughs
Lay stripped upon the ground:
Pale carnage beneath bright mist.

Gentildonna

She passed and left no quiver in the veins, who now
Moving among the trees, and clinging
                    in the air she severed,
Fanning the grass she walked on then, endures:
Grey olive leaves beneath a rain-cold sky.

(*Selected Poems*, p. 46)

The last lines, so similar in their construction, are very characteristic of Pound's 'Imagist' style. Having set up a scene or event, full of complex suggestiveness, he clinches the experience in a line that simply sets one object beside another: 'Pale carnage beneath bright mist', 'Grey olive leaves beneath a rain-cold sky'. This particular trick of style remained with Pound long after he ceased to call himself an Imagist and is thus a minor legacy of Imagism.

The Imagist movement was a short-lived one, and it may be suggested that one reason for this was that the Imagist habit, or principle, of centering your poem on a *comparison*, or simple yoking-together of two items, proved in the long run rather constricting. Pound seems to have found it so and moved on to a kind of verse that allowed of larger structures. Indirectly, though, his Imagist manner (and not only his, but that of one or two of his fellow-Imagists, such as 'H.D.') was of considerable and lasting influence. One can, I think, trace this influence in Eliot, and again in the American poet William Carlos Williams, and moreover in poems that do not, in point of fact, depend upon a comparison or any likening of this to that. One can detect the Imagist style – a hesitant, impeded motion, as if there were great gulfs of air or silence round each word or phrase – in this, from Eliot's *The Waste Land*:

> The river sweats
> Oil and tar
> The barges drift
> With the turning tide
> Red Sails
> Wide
> To leeward, swing on the heavy spar.
> The barges wash
> Drifting logs
> Down Greenwich reach
> Past the Isle of Dogs.[7]

One can perhaps detect it also – again partly as a matter of a particular *motion* – in the total simplicity and objectivity of this by William Carlos Williams:

> **Poem**
>
> As the cat
> climbed over
> the top of
>
> the jam closet
> first the right
> forefoot
>
> carefully
> then the hind
> stepped down
>
> into the pit of
> the empty
> flowerpot[8]

3. Early Poems

We may now explore more widely in Pound's earlier work, examining some rather diverse poems and groups of poems. I shall begin with the following group: 'The Spring'; ' "Ione, Dead the Long Year" '; 'Gentildonna'; and 'Liu Ch'e'. They are all from his collection *Lustra*, published in 1916, and you will find them in *Selected Poems* (pp. 43, 54, 46, 49). I have already discussed 'Gentildonna', but could you now read the others? What do you think they have in common?

DISCUSSION

In all four poems a human figure, a girl or a woman, has departed from the scene, yet still, in a sense, inhabits it, as a lingering presence – a trace, a memory or an aroma. Do the poems also have an emotion in common? For instance, shall we call them 'laments' or 'elegies'? 'Liu Ch'e' and 'Ione' certainly seem to be elegies. But if so, they are not very personal elegies. In 'Liu Ch'e' the phrase 'She the rejoicer of the heart' seems deliberately to evoke an 'ancient Chinese' note – this, we vaguely imagine, represents the stiff language of ancient mandarin courtesy – so that the death and loss are held at a distance from us. The poem ' "Ione, Dead the Long Year" ', too, sounds as though it might be a translation from an ancient Greek elegy, so again it is distanced from our feelings. Certainly 'Ione', in its opening lines, has a very lamenting cadence, a little reminiscent of the psalms. Yet we gather so little about Ione – only that she 'walked' – that we wonder if grief is the predominant emotion. In fact, prompted by the likeness to 'The Spring' and 'Gentildonna' – if I am right in seeing a likeness – one might wonder whether it is the heart that is involved so much as the senses and nervous system. Does not what is described in these poems resemble, a little, the phenomenon of 'after images' – the spectra that one 'sees' with closed eyes after viewing bright objects? In 'The Spring' Pound certainly seems much concerned with visualization. The poem calls to mind Botticelli's *Primavera*, and, as in Botticelli's painting, the landscape that the nymphs and goddesses are moving against is very vividly detailed. The phrase 'the bright tips' and the technical term 'vine-stock' makes us work hard at picturing not merely ornamental foliage but actual vines – and the naming of 'cyclamen' carried this process on. Thus, the 'tenuous ghost' lingering in the landscape seems to have a certain physical and material quality; the 'She', we feel, lives on not merely in the heart but in the optical memory.

I have been forcing a card on you in this discussion, for the point I wanted to get across is that Pound had a very special theory of memory. He regarded active, creative memory as a very different thing from a mere passive, camera-like recording of snapshots. He thought of beautiful things perceived and held alive in the memory as akin to myths or 'gods'. Here is how he spoke in an early essay 'Psychology and the Troubadours';

> I believe in a sort of permanent basis in humanity, that is to say, I believe that Greek myth arose when someone having passed through delightful psychic experience tried to communicate it to others and found it necessary to screen himself from persecution. Speaking aesthetically the myths are explications of mood; you may stop there or you may probe deeper.
>
> Certain it is that these myths are only intelligible in a vivid and glittering sense to those people to whom they occur. I know, I mean, one man who understands Persephone and Demeter, and one who understands the Laurel, and another who has, I should say, met Artemis. These things are for them *real*.[1]

'Delightful psychic experiences' seems a good phrase to describe 'The Spring' and 'Gentildonna' – and perhaps 'Ione' and 'Liu Ch'e' too, for all that they are elegies. Pound, indeed, is doing what he says the Greeks did and is inventing myths to clothe his 'delightful psychic experiences'.

Pound's poem 'The Spring' is, in fact, based upon a Greek fragment by the Cretan poet Ibycus, but based in a very strange and Poundian way. The fragment is fairly obscure anyway, and scholars disagree about its meaning. There is a word in it, *malides*, for instance, which may mean a kind of fruit tree, or alternatively 'nymphs who protect flocks'. Pound's reaction to this difficulty is to coin a word 'Maelids', to mean 'apple-nymphs', thus inventing a word not known to Greek dictionaries and a kind of nymph not known in Greek mythology. He has, that is to say, created a myth.

(He was sufficiently pleased with his 'Maelids' to reintroduce them in *The Cantos*.)

As we shall see, what he did with Ibycus's fragment is intensely characteristic of Pound and represents an entirely new approach to translation. (As you might say, he capitalized on his ignorance.) (He possessed a rough and inaccurate knowledge of a number of languages, but he let his imagination run on ahead of his knowledge.) (He was accustomed to enjoying foreign poems long before he fully understood them (Eliot, by the way, did the same, according to his own account). In a case such as the Ibycus one, his method was to stare at the foreign words with half-closed eyes, till an original English poem assembled itself from the débris.

There will be much to say about Pound and translation, but meanwhile let us go back to 'The Spring'. How would you describe what the poem is *saying*? What emotion is it expressing? Is it a sad poem, a cheerful poem, or just a picturesque poem not expressing any very positive human emotion? And why is the poet's heart 'bewildered'? What were your reactions?

DISCUSSION

I would say that it was a predominantly cheerful poem, a poem of cheerful pity. The poet savours the 'bewilderment' brought by a new spring; he is braced, invigorated, his body and mind brought to life by it, so that the emotions of last year must give way to those of the new one. He looks back on those old emotions, and those who gave rise to them, with a pity for those who cannot share in the new seasonal life. You could read the last three lines differently, of course, and as saying, 'All nature has its losses restored; only I am left inconsolable, having lost the woman who can never be replaced'. It would be a very traditional sentiment for an elegy. My own reading of the lines makes them subtler and less traditional. The poet's emotion seems to me to be a delicate compunction at remembering sentiments that one no longer feels, or will soon no longer feel. Pound, through his eccentric approach to translation, has found in his material a subtle and original feeling such as probably no poet has defined before.

All the poems we have just been discussing are in free verse, and this is a convenient moment for a digression on the nature of free verse. (One of the important contributions of the French *Symboliste* poets of the late nineteenth century (and in particular Jules Laforgue (1860–87)) was *vers libre* or 'free verse': verse, that is to say, which breaks the bonds of traditional versification.) Free

verse was not the invention of the *Symbolistes*; there was, for
instance, the powerful example of Walt Whitman, whose *Leaves of
Grass* (1855) is perhaps the most ambitious of all enterprises in free
verse. Nevertheless it was the *Symbolistes* who worked out a theory
or rationale for free verse, and their influence was long-lasting.
Most 'Imagist' poetry was written in free verse; indeed it is hard to
imagine it being written in traditional metre or rhyme. You will
remember Pound's advice (p. 13): 'As regarding rhythm: to
compose in sequence of the musical phrase, not in sequence of a
metronome'. Much of Eliot's work is in free verse, and so is the
most important work in verse of D.H. Lawrence. Eliot suggests a
helpful distinction in some 'Reflections on *Vers Libre*':

> . . . the most interesting [free] verse which has yet been written in our
> language has been done either by taking a very simple form, like the
> iambic pentameter, and constantly withdrawing from it, or taking no
> form at all and constantly approximating to a very simple one. It is
> this contrast between fixity and flux, this unperceived evasion of
> monotony, which is the very life of verse.[2]

> We may therefore formulate as follows: the ghost of some simple
> metre should lurk behind the arras in even the 'free-est' verse; to
> advance menacingly as we doze, and withdraw as we rouse. Or,
> freedom is only freedom when it appears against the background of
> an artificial limitation.

Let us look at ' "Ione, Dead the Long Year" '. To which of Eliot's
two categories of free verse would you say that it belonged? Is it
verse that takes a metrical norm and recedes from it, or is it verse
that is in no metrical form but converges upon metre?

'Ione, Dead the Long Year'

Empty are the ways,
Empty are the ways of this land
And the flowers
      Bend over with heavy heads.
They bend in vain.
Empty are the ways of this land
            Where Ione
Walked once, and now does not walk
But seems like a person just gone.

               (*Selected Poems*, p. 54)

DISCUSSION

I would say the second. I would say so with a very faint hesitation,
because it is so obviously verse, so obviously fashioned throughout
for musical effect; there are none of the loose and more-or-less

unmusical prose-rhythms we find in Walt Whitman. Nevertheless the music of the poem seems to be created for *this* poem alone and not to be related to any of the standard metres of English verse, so that puts it firmly in the second category.

Notice how the poem is held together by repetition of various kinds. There is repetition of rhythmic *motifs*. For instance 'are the ways', 'And the flowers' (one could pronounce 'flowers' as one long syllable), and 'Where Ione' have roughly the same rhythm and are obviously meant to echo one another. This kind of repetition works together with the actual repetition of words and phrases: 'Empty are the ways, Empty are the ways . . .' And speaking still of the shape or 'architecture' of the poem, the poem illustrates a general principle of free verse, that the unit of verse is the *line*. Free verse almost never runs over from the end of one line to the beginning of the next, as blank verse constantly does. If we were reading 'Ione' as prose, we would go straight on from 'Where Ione' to 'Walked once', but here we are not tempted to. We make a heavy pause after 'Where Ione', and during this pause all sorts of half-formed thoughts and emotions invade our minds.

What would one say about the diction or language or the poem? Is it striking in any way? Perhaps it is so only in being so plain and unremarkable. There is not a single 'poetical' word, but also, no word that draws attention to itself in any way.

What could one say was the meaning of the poem? What does it say? What emotion does it express? Sometimes this question is the one we should leave to the very last, and I think 'Ione' is a case in point. There is another question I would want to ask first, and that is, what is the *tone* of the poem? And does it have the same tone throughout?

For myself, I find a change of tone at a certain point of the poem. Having continued for much of its length in a solemn and almost liturgical tone of lament, the poem modulates, in the last two lines, into the tone of common speech. With 'Walked once, and now does not walk' we seem to move, imperceptibly, away from impersonal lament towards personal feeling. This is how a pang of personal grief and loss might come across the heart; 'it is as simple as that: she used to walk here and now does so no longer'. The change of tone is only faint, but it prepares the way for the last line, which transforms the poem. In all the earlier part the poet has been *overstating* grief: to picture flowers as bowing down their heads to find traces of a lost woman is extravagant and hyperbolic – this is the tone of exaggeration in which a nation mourns a lost hero or a lost homeland. In the last line, on the contrary, the poet *understates*, which is how we behave when moved by a private and personal loss. One could say nothing more commonplace and matter-of-fact or – ostensibly – more unemotional than 'But seems like a person just gone', and by its very understatement it suggests an immensity of loss.

Notice, finally, that the poem, like 'The Spring', appears to be mythological and legendary. We imagine that Ione must be a girl or goddess out of Homer or Ovid and that Pound is perhaps translating from some traditional Greek lamentation. In point of fact, 'Ione' was a name made up for a girl by the Victorian poet Landor, as an improvement on her real one – Miss Jones! But the poem truly *is* mythological in the Poundian sense.

Another poem, 'The Return' (from *Ripostes*, 1912, *Selected Poems*, p. 39) enforces this point. One feels sure that the poem must be referring to some well-known incident, real or mythological; perhaps it was a battle, and it is by a metaphor that the defeated warriors are described as 'gods' with 'silver hounds'. Yet Pound's source, if he had one, does not seem to be known, and it would probably not help us if it were. For the poem is all the more effective through our not knowing exactly, in the ordinary sense, what it is about. Donald Davie speculates, half-seriously, whether it might be about 'The decay of classical studies' or 'The etiolation of Hellenism as an artistic stimulus'.³ Hugh Kenner says that it is about 'the mode of divine apparitions in poetry'. But, in truth, the poem justifies the modernists' ambition that their poems should not have to be 'about' anything at all, but simply exist in their own right.

It is, I think, a hauntingly beautiful poem, much of its beauty lying in its musical organization – the subtleties of its elusive, hesitant, continually-varying movement (reinforced by the irregular laying-out of the poem on the printed page). It is a movement far away from traditional English metre, though full of hints and suggestions of classical metres: Pound certainly has 'broken the pentameter', as was his ambition'.⁵ And, after all, one has no difficulty in recognizing this 'return', this nerveless falling-back after a triumphant sallying-forth, as the pattern of an experience, an experience one has known somewhere, sometime, or often – though where, in what sphere of being, one cannot say. Thus to speak of Pound as having created a 'myth' is not too extravagant a way of talking.

Will you now read another poem of a type which, as we shall see, is deeply characteristic of Pound in that it involves the adoption of a 'mask', or *invented persona,* the poem 'Sestina: Altaforte', published in the collection *Exultations* in 1909 (*Selected Poems*, p.20).

DISCUSSION

A few facts about it: in form it is a 'sestina', that is to say a poem of six stanzas of six lines each, in which the same line endings reappear in each stanza but in a different order, followed by an 'envoi' or shorter concluding section. The form was invented by the Provençal poet or 'troubadour' Arnaut Daniel (c. 1180–1210), and the speaker in the poem is another Provençal troubadour, Bertran de Born (Viscount of Hautefort). The poem, in fact, is a free version of a poem by Bertran in praise of war – though Bertran's poem is not in sestina form itself. The troubadours flourished in southern France, Spain and Italy in the eleventh, twelfth and thirteenth centuries and were frequently, though not always, men of high rank, like Bertran de Born, and would retain a 'jongleur' or minstrel to sing their songs. (Bertran's poem is unusual in its subject matter: the favourite theme of the troubadours was love – a love conducted according to a 'courtly' convention which was a parody of feudal service and religious devotion.)

It is a poem I can imagine different people reacting to very differently. I can picture someone disliking it as a tawdry piece of sham-medievalism. I like it a lot myself, however, and I will try to say why. It seems to me a triumph of *style*. I mean by this that Pound has decided to throw in the vividest medieval colour he has in his palette: colourfulness of diction, colourfulness of attitude, 'colourfulness' or sumptuousness of sound patterns. No one could say that the poem does not have flavour; but it is not just a disorganized riot of flavour and colour: Pound has selected a diction – full of vigorous monosyllables: 'stinks', 'clash', 'stour' (conflict), 'bawds', 'sluts' etc. – which seems to consort and hang together. It is mainly a Saxon vocabulary, and this may seem surprising, since these are feudal times, to which Norman words, at any rate in the case of a feudal lord, would be more appropriate. But Bertran's Provençal has a clipped, clanging, vigorous ring very unlike the slithery and nasal refinement of modern French, and, as Pound has seen, the closest English parallel to this contrast is the contrast between the Saxon, and the Norman or Latin, elements in our vocabulary. He points up the contrast by balancing his vigorous monosyllables against Latinate-sounding disyllables: 'rejoicing', 'opposing'. He does this particularly in his line endings, and since these line endings are six times repeated, the effect is rubbed in. Altogether, because of the sestina form, one becomes very familiar with Pound's chosen 'Bertran' vocabulary.

Note Pound's first line. 'Damn it all!' 'Damn it all!' is Victorian or twentieth-century slang, and by means of it Pound, at the very start, has let us know that his sham-medievalism is not meant to take us in. This is a delicate piece of honesty on his part, which, having performed once, he does not need to repeat.

Not only has Pound created a special 'Bertran' vocabulary; he also invented a very special rhythmic movement for the poem. It is apparently a five-foot line; but if so, it is one very unlike the ordinary iambic pentameter. His lines tend to grind to an abrupt halt or hiatus somewhere in mid-course, bringing the reader up short: for instance that hiatus between 'Papiols, come!' and 'Let's to music!' in stanza 1. The reader is stopped dead by it and has to take a new breath before proceeding. On the other hand this *is* a single five-foot line; it does not work like alliterative verse (for instance the verse of *Piers Plowman*) where the line breaks into two independent parts. Pound's line, despite its jolting hiatus, has to be read as a single unit. The effect of this rhythmic movement, varying as it does from line to line, is to make those strong monosyllables clang and percuss together, in a way surely very expressive of a warlike subject matter.

Pound, so far as I know, was the inventor of this particular rhythmic effect, but he did not use it much again. The poem strikes me as a brilliant young man's poem, done partly for the fun of the thing. He was fond of reading it aloud at the top of his voice, and when he and his friends sat down to table in their favourite restaurant, the waiters hurried to put screens around them.

Next, I would like to consider 'Cino' and 'Pierre Vidal Old'. 'Cino' was published in 1908, in Pound's first collection *A Lume Spento*, and 'Pierre Vidal Old' in *Exultations* (1909), so they belong roughly to the same period as 'Sestina: Altaforte'. Like that, too, they are imaginary soliloquies by troubadour poets. I would like you to read these poems now (*Selected Poems*, pp. 15, 32).

If you are not familiar with Pound's impressionistic methods, these poems, especially 'Cino', may strike you are obscure in places, and I will offer a little in the way of explication. The main drift of 'Cino' is clear, I think. Cino is an Italian troubadour, wandering in exile from his native city and reflecting cynically and bitterly about the high-born ladies who used to enjoy his verses and praises but did not take him seriously as a lover. He imagines them as remembering him from time to time, with affection, or as discussing him with pretended indifference with their noble suitors. But, really, they knew nothing about him – they were not even sure if the songs he sang were his own (or, as you might say, whether he was a troubadour or a jongleur). He tells himself he will forget the worthless creatures and sing of the sun and the clouds of heaven, but thoughts of them keep creeping back. Finally he does sing a hymn to the sun, a comic parody of such a hymn, in three languages, burlesquing the learning that the ladies, probably, would never have suspected on the part of such a 'vagabond'.

The sense of 'Lips, words, and you snare them ... souls of song' is not very clear, but I would take it to mean that the ladies are only material for songs and better forgotten otherwise. The word 'sinistro' means 'ill-omened', but also 'bastard (i.e. illegitimate): Pound is using the Italian word 'sinistro' in the sense of a bar sinister in heraldry, signifying illegitimacy. Cino means that if the truth were told the lord has no more right to his estates than Cino himself. 'Pollo Phoibee' is Phoebus Apollo, the Greek god who in one aspect is identified with the sun. The German 'Wanderlied' means 'song of a rover'.

'Pierre Vidal' does not offer difficulties to the same degree, though it is important to know that Pierre Vidal was a real person and a well-known troubadour – Pound, however, having altered the facts of his life for his own purposes.

'Cino' and 'Pierre Vidal Old' are both strongly influenced by Robert Browning. It was, in fact, from Browning that Pound learned this whole notion of plunging the reader, without explanation, into the life and thoughts of some figure of the past, as he ruminates and monologizes to himself or to a listener. It is a way of writing a play or novel without the usual scaffolding of such. I will quote one of Browning's dramatic monologues for comparison.

My Last Duchess

FERRARA

That's my last Duchess painted on the wall,
Looking as if she were alive. I call
That piece a wonder, now: Frà Pandolf's hands
Worked busily a day, and there she stands.
Will't please you sit and look at her? I said
'Frà Pandolf' by design, for never read
Strangers like you that pictured countenance,
The depth and passion of its earnest glance,
But to myself they turned (since none puts by
The curtains I have drawn for you, but I)
And seemed as they would ask me, if they durst,
How such a glance came there; so, not the first

Are you to turn and ask thus. Sir, 'twas not
Her husband's presence only, called that spot
Of joy into the Duchess' cheek: perhaps
Frà Pandolf chanced to say 'Her mantle laps
'Over my lady's wrist too much', or 'Paint
'Must never hope to reproduce the faint
'Half-flush that dies along her throat:' such stuff
Was courtesy, she thought, and cause enough
For calling up that spot of joy. She had
A heart – how shall I say? – too soon made glad,
Too easily impressed; she liked whate'er
She looked on, and her looks went everywhere.
Sir, 'twas all one! My favour at her breast,
The dropping of the daylight in the West,
The bough of cherries some officious fool
Broke in the orchard for her, the white mule
She rode with round the terrace – all and each
Would draw from her alike the approving speech,
Or blush, at least. She thanked men, – good! but thanked
Somehow – I know not how – as if she ranked
My gift of a nine-hundred-years-old name
With anybody's gift. Who'd stoop to blame
This sort of trifling? Even had you skill
In speech – (which I have not) – to make your will
Quite clear to such a one, and say, 'Just this
'Or that in you disgusts me; here you miss,
'Or there exceed the mark' – and if she let
Herself be lessoned so, nor plainly set
Her wits to yours, forsooth, and made excuse,
– E'en then would be some stooping; and I choose
Never to stoop. Oh sir, she smiled, no doubt,
Whene'er I passed her; but who passed without
Much the same smile? This grew; I gave commands;
Then all smiles stopped together. There she stands
As if alive. Will't please you rise? We'll meet
The company below, then. I repeat,
The Count your master's known munificence
Is ample warrant that no just pretence
Of mine for dowry will be disallowed;
Though his fair daughter's self, as I avowed
At starting, is my object. Nay, we'll go
Together down, sir. Notice Neptune, though,
Taming a sea-horse, though a rarity,
Which Claus of Innsbruck cast in bronze for me!

The likeness is surely very plain? Indeed I would suggest that you
might almost imagine the stanza 'And conquered! . . .' in 'Pierre
Vidal Old' to be by Browning himself. This would not be true of the
first stanza, however (at least if we are judging Browning by 'My

Last Duchess'), for it is not a dramatic monologue, such as you might get in a play, but rather a stanza from an imaginary song or poem by Pierre Vidal.

The point this illustrates is that, in these poems about troubadours, Pound is doing two separate things. Sometimes he is presenting a character dramatically, at other times he is writing a poem such as the character might have written. He is moving between the two poles of drama (or fiction) and translation. 'Sestina: Altaforte' is, as we have seen, a translation, though with dramatic overtones. 'Pierre Vidal Old', for much of the time, reads like an imaginary Provençal poem, but it glides out of this into Browningesque dramatic monologue, and eventually, in the last two lines, it becomes a drama with stage directions. 'Cino' is a mixture of all sorts of things: Browningesque dramatic monologue, medieval lyric, and witty twentieth-century burlesque ('Pollo Phoibee, old tin pan, you . . .').

The poet who wrote these three poems (in 1908 or thereabouts) is very different from the one who, two or three years later, was to preach 'Direct treatment of the "thing", whether subjective or objective' and to recommend 'To use absolutely no word that does not contribute to the presentation'. Or is he? It is worth speculating what the later Pound would have said about these poems. Presumably the Pound of the Imagist period would have thought a stanza such as this from 'Pierre Vidal Old'

> Stark, keen, triumphant, till it plays at death.
> God! she was white then, splendid as some tomb
> High wrought of marble, and the panting breath
> Ceased utterly. Well, then I waited, drew,
> Half-sheathed, then naked from its saffron sheath
> Drew full this dagger that doth tremble here.
>
> (*Selected Poems*, p. 33)

too wordy, too rhetorical, too Victorian, even allowing that it is, supposedly, Pierre Vidal speaking, not Pound. As for 'Cino', Pound expressed dissatisfaction at the time of writing it. ' "Cino" – the thing is banal. He might be anyone', he wrote to his fellow-poet William Carlos Williams in 1908. This suggests that, by his later standards, what the poem fails to do is – by means of word play, metaphor, rhythm and 'music' – to focus something unique. Cino 'might be anyone': he is not, like Shakespeare's Othello, someone whom we recognize as that man, and that man alone, in every word he says.

In imagining what more Pound the Imagist would have said about 'Cino', I am not trying to argue against the poem, which

seems to me a fine and original one. A good way in to 'Cino' – that
is to say to coming to a judgement of it – is to ask yourself if its
obscurities are all justified. Why is it obscure? Partly, certainly,
because Pound wants to cut away all unpoetic linking matter. He
wants to be free to make lightning-quick transitions from one bit of
Cino's thought and experience to another. And, one must admit,
there is a great deal in the poem, in a concentrated form: period
flavour and language, lyrical song, dramatized reminiscence,
literary burlesque and novelistic self-revelation. But, one must ask,
do the allusions and transitions all work? Or has Pound, perhaps,
botched some of them – performed them in an impatient and
careless way, thus creating unnecessary obscurities?

There is another reason for invoking the later Pound here, and
that is that these poems, and others related to them – 'La Fraisne',
'Na Audiart', 'Marvoil', and 'A Villonaud: Ballad of the Gibbet' –
represent early experiments on Pound's part in a genre which
assumed even greater importance for him later on: I mean, the
'mask' or *persona*. It was a belief shared by Pound with other
'modernists', including Yeats and Eliot, that good poetry is
impersonal and works by indirect means. The poet is not a man or
woman speaking directly to a listener, offering the spectacle of the
poet's personality and emotions. This is how the Romantic poet, or
one type of Romantic poet – the Shelleyan kind – thought of
himself; and the 'modernists' united in distrusting Romanticism. In
their view, the poet should stand aloof from his poem. ('All that is
personal soon rots', wrote Yeats, 'it must be packed in ice and
salt.'[6]) According to this view, the poet should not try to evoke
emotion directly, but should interpose something between self and
the reader, leaving it to this to evoke emotion. The poet should
conceal and obliterate the self. This may be done by presenting
objects without comment, as in Imagism. But another way is by
donning a 'mask' or 'persona', a face not the poet's own. Ezra
Pound at different stages of his career adopted a whole series of
'masks' or impersonations, writing in the guise of a troubador poet,
or a classical Chinese lyricist, or a Roman elegist. He said in his
study of the sculptor Gaudier-Brzeska:

> In the 'search for oneself', in the search for 'sincere self-expression',
> one gropes, one finds some seeming verity. One says 'I am this, that,
> or the other', and with the words scarcely uttered one ceases to be
> that thing.
>
> I began this search for the real in a book called *Personae*, casting
> off, as it were, complete masks of the self in each poem. I continued
> in a long series of translations, which were but more elaborate
> masks.[7]

One may observe a common factor in the various characters which Pound has chosen as disguises in his early 'Provençal' period. Apart from the case of 'La Fraisne', they are all poets, like Pound himself; also poets suffering from various kinds of rejection and exclusion. Secondly, they are all poets who *lived* their poetry – even, in the case of Pierre Vidal, the poet of 'courtly love', to the extent of running mad for love and joining a wolf-pack. Pound is insistent upon this quality in his chosen personae: 'Villon's verse is real, because he lived it; as Bertran de Born, as Arnaut Marvoil, as that mad poseur Vidal, he lived it'.[8] And, we may guess, this was something Pound admired because he felt that a modern poet could *not* aspire to it.

It is a cardinal point in understanding Pound to realize how much his thoughts upon any subject began from or came back to the question of the poet and his role in society. He lived and dressed the part of the poet, in his own person – indeed in rather an old-fashioned way, with long hair and flowing ties, at a time when poets were beginning to dress like bank clerks – and this expressed his sense of dedication. Thus it is only natural that in 'the search for oneself' the masks he should have tried on should have been those of poets; and logical, too, that they should have been troubadours, for the troubadours did not so much compose poetry in order to succeed with women as cultivate women in order to have a subject for poetry.

There is more to his 'troubadour' poetry than that, however, and something subtler. As we have seen, Pound is doing two things at once in these poems; he veers between dramatic recreation in the Browning manner, and translation. And as he developed he came to feel that, of the two ways of restoring the past to life, the more effective was translation. So closely are poetic rhythms and turns of speech related to the nervous system, a modern poet could, he felt, resurrect the most intimate being of an ancient poet. We have already seen Pound at work as a 'translator' in his poem 'The Spring' and observed what a very long way his method lies from the usual idea of translation. When we go on to consider those three works of his maturity, *Cathay, Homage to Sextus Propertius* and *Hugh Selwyn Mauberley*, Pound's complex relationship to translation is going to loom large.

Meanwhile let us look at another group of poems, in effect, 'epigrams': 'Meditatio', 'The Bath Tub', 'Arides' and 'Ladies' (*Selected Poems*, pp. 51, 49). They were published in *Lustra* (1916) but were written somewhere about 1912, that is to say, three or four years after the 'troubadour' poems. It might be held that in them Pound is donning another 'mask', however I would not be inclined to use the word 'mask' about them myself. Clearly, Pound, in writing them, is pretending to be a certain class of person: an observer with a detached and ironic eye for the follies of his fellow men and women; but we do not visualize this person very precisely. He is more of a generalized pose than a flesh-and-blood individual. The main *raison d'être* of the poems, I suggest, is the practising of a certain tone of voice. How would one define Pound's tone in them? Amused, drily satirical, mock literary – i.e. withdrawing from everyday speech into formal or 'literary' language for ironic effect? Are they bitter or cruel – say, like the satires on women that Cino might have written? I would be inclined to say no, on the contrary rather genial. Above all, *poised*, going in for a certain kind of aplomb. Pound is exploring the resources of a pose of imperturbability, such that the phenomena of human life may cause its possessor to raise any eyebrow, but not disturb him in any deeper way. It is a poise and tone and voice we shall find him exploiting in more serious poems later.

Now let us consider another group that we could call 'poems of affirmation': 'Commission', 'The Garret', 'Salutation', 'Salutation the Second', 'The Rest', belonging to much the same period. What would you say they are about, from the point of view of subject matter? Is Pound making any use of 'masks' in them?

DISCUSSION

It seems to me the answer is no, and what we have here is a poet meeting the reader more than half way and speaking very openly of what he believes. Perhaps there is a little posturing and taking-up-of-attitudes in lines such as 'Take thought;/I have weathered the storm,/I have beaten out my exile,' But if so, the posturing is of a transparent kind.

There is, in fact, an 'influence', I think, and that it Walt Whitman, whose poems ran to lists and catalogues in much the same way as 'Commission': for instance this extract from 'Song of the Open Road'.

I inhale great draughts of space,
The east and the west are mine, and the north and the south are
    mine.

I am larger, better than I thought,
I did not know I held so much goodness.

All seems beautiful to me,
I can repeat over to men and women You have done such good to me
  I would do the same to you,
I will recruit for myself and you as I go,
I will scatter myself among men and women as I go,
I will toss a new gladness and roughness among them,
Whoever denies me it shall not trouble me,
Whoever accepts me he or she shall be blessed and shall bless me.[9]

The significance of Whitman for Pound was, precisely, that he spoke out plainly, perhaps more plainly than any poet has done before.

These are not likely to strike you as Pound's best poems, and – if you are not a Whitman – perhaps you can say more in poetry by indirect suggestion than by plain speaking. Nevertheless, these poems seem to me far from negligible.

My own feeling is that 'Commission' begins to be effective and original somewhere about its third stanza. The metaphors in this stanza are rather a medley, but with their aid one feels that something important is being defined, something less obvious and generalized than the doctrines of the earlier sections. What this 'something', this belief, constitutes, is of importance in understanding Pound the man. He was a tough fighter and battled for freedom – freedom from 'the system', from social convention, from economic slavery – in a robust and swashbuckling manner; but the freedom he was claiming was the freedom to be sensitive, to stretch out the most delicate tentacles of the spirit.

Altogether we can accept 'Commission' as a fair account of Pound's social and political views at this time – views not so very different from those of other radical thinkers, for instance Bernard Shaw, except in the important respect that at the centre of all his social thinking was 'Art'; new art, for him, was the true engine of social and moral salvation. He explained on the flyleaf of *Lustra* that a *lustrum* was 'an offering for the sins of the whole people, made by the censors at the expiration of their five years of office'. It was not said quite ironically. Pound felt that in these London years he had taken the responsibility for English literary life upon his shoulders; and a time was to come when he would call himself a fool for his pains.

4. Cathay

I have described Pound's 'Imagist' period as the climax of his early career. We should remember, though, that it was a fairly brief episode, lasting – shall we say – from 1910 or 1911 to 1914. Why he swung away from Imagism is a complex matter, but one major factor was an historical accident. It so happened that in 1913 Pound met the widow of Ernest Fenollosa, an American of Spanish descent who had been one of the first Western scholars recruited by the newly-founded University of Tokyo and who, as well as publishing various books on oriental art and literature, left a large mass of unpublished notes on these subjects. Mrs Fenollosa, since her husband's death in 1908, had been searching for someone who might make use of his material, and having admired some poems of Pound's and being moreover impressed by his interest in Fenollosa's researches, she gave the manuscripts into his keeping and appointed him literary executor.

For Pound the Fenollosa notes were a revelation. Fenollosa had worked both on Japanese literature, especially the Japanese 'Noh' plays, and on classical Chinese poetry. He had employed Japanese scholars to assist him, and among his papers were numerous word-for-word 'cribs' to Japanese and Chinese plays and poems, together with his attempts to work them up into literary translations. There was also an essay on 'The Chinese Written Character as a Medium for Poetry', finding in the special characteristics of Chinese as a literary language the basis for a new theory of language and of poetry in general. Pound, though he knew no Chinese or Japanese, quickly perceived all sorts of new possibilities and lessons for English literature in this material.

Written Chinese possesses no letters of the alphabet, as in Western languages, but rather ideograms or 'characters' standing

for complete words: for instance 日 meaning sun, and 月 meaning moon. And these characters are also combined to form further

words: thus 明 meaning bright. In tackling a Chinese poem

Fenollosa's method was, in the first place, to get his teacher to supply him with a gloss for each character in the poem, the result looking like this:

blue	blue	river	bank	grass
luxuriantly	luxuriantly	garden	in	willow
fill	fill	storied house	on	girl
(white	(white	just	window	door
(brilliant	(brilliant			
(luminous	(luminous			
beauty of face	beauty of face	red	powder	toilet
slender	slender	put forth	white	hand
in former times	was	courtesan	house	girl
now	is	dissipated	son's	wife
dissipated	son	go away	not	return
empty	bed	hard	only one, alone	keep

He would then experiment with turning this into conventional English, which meant adding the kind of logical and explanatory sentence-structure we are accustomed to in English. <u>What struck Pound immediately, however, was that, in a way, the bare bones of the Chinese poem were a realization of what Imagism had been aiming at – a poetry, as far as possible, that presented and juxtaposed 'things' without explanation or connecting matter.</u> Evidently, our language being what it is, one could not write quite like this in English, but the fact that it was possible in Chinese was an unexpected vindication of Imagist doctrine.

Other qualities in Chinese verse appealed to him too and pointed in the same direction. <u>Chinese poetry was frequently a poetry of understatement: the poet would merely present a situation, as concisely as possible, and leave it to the reader to infer the emotional implication. Again, it used natural scenes and backgrounds to render feeling and mood in the way that seemed proper to Pound, that is to say an economical</u> – or as you might say 'mathematical' – way, providing an 'equation' for the mood. It did not 'go on' about nature as Georgian poets tend to do.

Further, in Fenollosa's essay on the Chinese written character, Pound found a theory, which confirmed certain doubts of his own about Imagism. According to Fenollosa:

The sentence form was forced upon primitive men by nature itself. It was not we who made it; it was a reflection of the temporal order in causation. All truth has to be expressed in sentences because all truth is the *transference* of power. The type of sentence in nature is a flash of lightning. It passes between two terms, a cloud and the earth . . . The form of the Chinese transitive sentence, and of the English (omitting particles), exactly corresponds to this universal form of action in nature. (This brings language close to *things*, and in its strong reliance upon verbs it erects all speech into a kind of dramatic poetry.[1])

Applying this to English, he went on:

. . .the great strength of our language lies in its splendid array of transitive verbs, drawn both from Anglo-Saxon and from Latin sources. These give us the most individual characterisations of force. The power lies in their recognition of nature as a vast storehouse of forces. We do not say in English that things seem, or appear, or eventuate, or even that they are; but that they *do* . . . I had to discover for myself why Shakespeare's English was so immeasurably superior to all others. I found that it was his persistent, natural and magnificent use of hundreds of transitive verbs. Rarely will you find an 'is' in his sentences.[2]

Fenollosa's theory is based, partly, on a misunderstanding of the Chinese written language, one that Pound was to share. (Like other language-theorists before them, they tended to find in Chinese what they wanted to find, and they persuaded themselves that the basic principle of the Chinese written language was that the characters stood not for sounds, as in English, but for *things*.) And indeed it is true that a relatively small class of Chinese characters do their 象形 指事

signifying without reference to spoken sound: thus 人 signifies 'man', and 信 (man + word) signifies 'sincere'. However, the

truth is, the great majority of Chinese characters do in fact 形聲 represent spoken sounds. Thus, to take an example given by Hugh Kenner (*The Pound Era*, pp.227–8), the right-hand side of the

character 訪 tells us to say *fang*, a syllable that has various

different possible meanings – 'square', 'distinct', 'spin', 'ask', 'room', 'kettle', 'board' – and the left-hand side of the character,

言 i.e. 'speak', tells us that we are dealing with the meaning of

fang appropriate to speech. Thus the whole character means 'ask'.

Fenollosa's notion is not thereby discredited as a theory of poetry, and for Pound it came as a powerful criticism of the principles of Imagism. The implications, as he saw them, were that Imagism took too static a view of what poetry could perform. It conceived of the world as so many inert 'things', to be brought into juxtaposition, whereas the world is made up of *energies*, and a poem should be a sort of 'vortex' concentrating these energies.

Such an idea had been in Pound's mind for some time, but it seems to have been Fenollosa's essay that brought it into focus, and the word 'vortex', which he now coined as a literary term, had a brief but spectacular career. In the early days of 1914 he was closely associated with the painter and writer Wyndham Lewis, who was producing a new, very *avant-garde* magazine called *Blast*. The easiest way to taste the flavour of *Blast* is to look at the advertisement for it published in April 1914 and reproduced below. The notion now came to Pound, on the eve of the first issue of *Blast*, of christening the new movement it represented by the name of 'Vorticism'. 'Vorticism' was to be the English version of abstract art, with Wyndham Lewis as the leading Vorticist painter, Henri Gaudier-Brzeska as its leading sculptor, and Pound himself as its leading poet.

Vorticism was a short-lived movement, and I have not space to trace its history here. What I am more interested in is the general significance of the year 1914 in Pound's career. With the new light from China and with the launching of Vorticism in the arts there seemed to Pound to be the materials of a second Renaissance. But as we cannot but remember, 1914 was the year of an even larger event, the outbreak of the First World War. The war disrupted Vorticism and made a mockery of Pound's imagined Renaissance, and the rest of his career was to be coloured by the disappointment of his hopes of 1914.[3]

As far as Pound's own verse is concerned, the influence of Fenollosa's theory of poetry was a gradual and long-term one and is not fully visible till *The Cantos*. In more immediate terms, what Fenollosa's papers provided Pound with was the materials of a new 'mask', an oriental one; and combined with this, a new challenge to his powers of 'creative translation'. First of all he worked on Fenollosa's notes on Japanese 'Noh' drama, producing a number of translations (published in 1916 and 1917) and stimulating the interest of Yeats in 'Noh' drama. Pound then turned to the Chinese poets, and the fruit of this was the translation published in 1915 as *Cathay*.

It would be a good idea at this point to read through the *Cathay* poems once or twice (*Selected Poems*, pp.64–78). One

READY APRIL

BLAST

EDITED BY
WYNDHAM LEWIS.

To be published Quarterly.   First Number will contain

MANIFESTO.

Story by Wyndham Lewis.

Poems by Ezra Pound.

Reproductions of Drawings, Paintings, and Sculpture
by
Etchells, Nevinson, Lewis, Hamilton, Brzeska, Wadsworth, Epstein, Roberts, etc., etc.

Twenty Illustrations.

Price 2s. 6d.   Annual Subscription 10s. 6d.
America 65 cents.   ,, $2.50.

Discussion of Cubism, Futurism, Imagisme and all Vital Forms of Modern Art.

THE CUBE.   THE PYRAMID.

Putrifaction of Guffaws Slain by Appearance of BLAST.

NO Pornography.   NO Old Pulp.

END OF THE CHRISTIAN ERA.

All Subscriptions should be addressed to BLAST, 4, Percy St., Tottenham Court Rd., London, W.C.   Cheques payable to " Blast."

Blast manifesto — designed by Wyndham Lewis

minor point of information: Pound mostly gives the names of
Chinese poets in the Japanese form, this being how Fenollosa
learned them from his Japanese teachers. (Thus *Rihaku* is the poet
better known as *Li Po*.) What is your general impression of these
poems? What is the effect of what might be called the 'Chinoiserie'
element in them? For example, in 'The River Song', and in 'Exile's
Letter'?

DISCUSSION

The collection, it will be agreed, has a very strong and homogeneous
flavour. My own impression of *Cathay* is of vast distances and of
the partings and exiles that distances entail; an empire so huge that
its defenders and functionaries cannot know its purposes – and
perhaps these purposes are absurd; distances also in time and
history, so great that human glory cannot hope to outlast them; and
set against these, the comforts that the reasonable man knows are
not absurd – wine, friendship and the private life: '. . . there is no
end of talking,/There is no end of things in the heart.' Hugh Kenner
has suggested that we should think of the poems as evoking the
1914–18 war, and there may be something in this, though perhaps
it was not in the forefront of Pound's mind. Here is how Kenner
puts it:

> Its exiled bowmen, deserted women, levelled dynasties, departures
> for far places, lonely frontier guardsmen and glories remembered
> from afar, cherished memories, were selected from the diverse wealth
> in the Fenollosa notebooks by a sensibility responsive to torn
> Belgium and disrupted London.[4]

One can easily imagine a critic who objected to *Cathay* as being
'sham-orientalism': the same kind of thing as willow-pattern plates
and the 'Chinese' screens you might find in seaside boarding-
houses. He or she might complain, for instance, that the opening
section of 'The River Song', or that business in 'Exile's Letter' of
someone buying someone else a 'special tavern', were just incomprehensible bits of Chinese 'colour'. I have helped my imaginary critic
by my examples, for 'The River Song' is, I would think, the most
baffling and remote of the poems in *Cathay*, and I do not myself
think it is a complete success. I can understand someone feeling
that, in those opening lines particularly, Pound is not doing much
more than go in for 'colour' and 'Chinoiserie'. Again, I am always
held up momentarily in 'Exile's Letter' by that business about the
tavern. I cannot imagine a set of circumstances in which someone
would buy a tavern for someone else to enjoy himself in. Reading it,

one thinks lamely, 'Well, it must have been in the original'; but this does not make it any better. However, by contrast, doesn't this one stumbling block – if you agree that it is a stumbling-block – bring into relief how very fine otherwise this poem is – fine as an English poem, whatever the original was like? What, I suggest, one sees in this poem, and in *Cathay* generally – and it shows Pound's mastery – is his controlling precisely the dose of exoticism or 'Chinoiserie' or incomprehensible Chinese 'colour' that there shall be in his poems. One of the originalities of his approach to translation is that he will not pretend that what he is writing is *not* a translation (and this is an attitude very much in accordance with 'modernist' principles). And on the other hand, isn't it exactly this honesty about what he is doing as translator that helps Pound produce a poem that comes home to us as an English poem? Consider, in line 24 of 'Exile's Letter', the boldness, the cheek, of rendering the word, which most translators would render as 'reed-pipe', by 'mouth-organ' – thus inevitably reminding us of those little tin-plated instruments we used to make dismal noises with as children. 'Reed-pipe' would not mean much to us; 'mouth-organ' means something quite precise and, presumably, wrong. Pound has chosen the second to make us sit up and register the suggestive, and faintly comic, contrast of Eastern and Western cultures. This, however, is the kind of trick he is careful not to play too often.

As far as we have reached in his career, I find 'Exile's Letter' the most impressive of Pound's 'masks' or personae and its concluding eleven lines extremely moving – also not in the least exotic:

> And once again, later, we met at the South bridge-head.
> And then the crowd broke up, you went north to San palace,
> And if you ask how I regret that parting:
> It is like the flowers falling at Spring's end
>   Confused, whirled in a tangle.
> What is the use of talking, and there is no end of talking,
> There is no end of things in the heart.
> I call in the boy,
> Have him sit on his knees here
>   To seal this,
> And send it a thousand miles, thinking.
>
> *Selected Poems*, p.72

Consider the last line of all. Is not that 'thinking' most touching, and a perfect example of the art of understatement? Pound has learned that art, in part at least, from Chinese poetry, in which understatement is a ruling principle: and so the idea that he is communicating Chinese poetry to us cannot be entirely false.

(T.S. Eliot said, with very Eliot-like ambiguity: 'it must be pointed out that Pound is the inventor of Chinese poetry for our time'.[5]) But of course, the main thing is that he has written a fine English poem, one in which – if you agree with Kenner, as I do – he has been able to make an oblique statement about human life and values from the standpoint of London in 1915.

Will you now re-read 'South-Folk in Cold Country'? (*Selected Poems*, p.74). What are your impressions of it? Do you notice any 'Chinoiserie' lines? And lines of strikingly contrasting effect? Try listing the varieties of line in the poem. And does the poem seem to you to have a structure? How does it hang together?

DISCUSSION

It is surely a surprise to find in the same poem such a line as 'Emotion is born out of habit', which sounds like a proverb, or a sage's pronouncement, together with the impressionistic and visually suggestive line, 'Mind and spirit drive on feathery banners'. And are not such contrasts characteristic? My list of the varieties of line would be: 'Chinoiserie' lines, i.e. lines like the first two, which you do not positively expect to understand; moral saws or maxims, such as 'Emotion is born out of habit'; the line 'Surprised. Desert turmoil. Sea sun' – a striking, somewhat cinematic, line, unlike any other in the poem; 'Imagist' lines, such as 'Lice swarm like ants over our accoutrements'; and the last three lines, for which I cannot precisely think of a description, but which recall Pound's 'The Return'. Altogether, it is a poem in which Pound has drawn fairly widely on the different styles we have seen him mastering.

The relation of the poem to its original is interesting. Actually, the line corresponding to 'Surprised. Desert turmoil. Sea sun' is more straightforward in the Chinese. It reads something like this:

Startling   sands   derange   sea   sun

This is untranslatable, because the 'sea' in question is really the Mongolian desert, which is known as 'the vast sea', an allusion incomprehensible to the Western reader. Pound has been forced to improvise, and his 'Surprised' is rather brilliant, combining the sense of 'startling' with the sense of surprised, i.e. taken unawares, by barbarian invaders. But what strikes me even more about the line is that it is as if Pound has decided to do an imitation of Chinese characters or 'ideograms'. One can easily imagine a Chinese character standing for 'surprised', another for 'desert turmoil' and another for 'sea sun'. This is a good example of his creative opportunism.

The form of Pound's poem depends very much on the continual springing of surprises, especially those surprising transitions from one kind of line to another. And what we should notice is that these effects would only be conceivable in free verse: it requires the flexibility of free verse to accommodate them. On the other hand, if we were ever tempted to think of free verse as 'formless', this poem should correct us: it is held together by all sorts of devices, as a piece of carpentry is held together by tenons and mortices. The first two lines:

> The Dai horse neighs against the bleak wind of Etsu,
> The birds of Etsu have no love for En, in the north,

are balanced by the fourth and fifth lines:

> Yesterday we went out of the Wild-Goose gate,
> Today from the Dragon-pen.

through having the same sort of tense structure and sentence structure. The third line:

> Emotion is born out of habit.

is balanced, to a certain degree, by the sixth line:

> Surprised. Desert turmoil. Sea sun.

if only because we feel them to have the same underlying three-stress rhythm. On the other hand, from another point of view, the sixth line is very different from the third: it is not a maxim, like 'Emotion is born out of habit'. The lines that 'Emotion is born out of habit' most resemble come later:

> Hard fight gets no reward.
> Loyalty is hard to explain.

One can read these lines as maxims or as brief expressions of a situation, terse with a soldier's restraint. Thus, as in carpentry, the components of the poem are locked together not by a single set of tensions but by several interacting ones.

I could go on, but shall not, and it would become boring if every time one wrote about a poem one spelt out all these details of structure. The point is, rather, that one should acquire the habit of noticing these matters instinctively, without having to bring them to the forefront of one's mind.

I would, however, like to compare the 'crib' of a Chinese poem by Mei Sheng which I quoted on p. 34 ('blue   blue   river   bank

grass' etc.) with the version that Pound made of it, 'The Beautiful
Toilet', (*Selected Poems*, p.65) and suggest the processes of Pound's
mind as he hewed an English poem out of the Chinese one. One
asks oneself, first, what was the point of breaking the poem into
two sections? This, is clearly important, for the two sections are
strikingly different. But different in what way? Would you now
read the poem?

DISCUSSION

The answer, I suggest, is that Pound has built his whole poem
round a change in tone of voice, coming after 'slender hand': he
begins in a lamenting, musical, romantically-evocative cadence, and
then with 'And she was a courtezan in the old days', he shifts to the
drily matter-of-fact. This curve of feeling, of course, has a general
kind of resemblance to the downward curve of the courtesan's life.

Note, next, how line 5 of the crib has found its way into the
title of the poem.

Then, a question that suggests itself is, does Pound's 'white,
white of face' suggest the same as the gloss 'White/brilliant/
luminous', and if not, why not? My answer would be that Pound
has seen dramatic possibilities in the 'White/brilliant/luminous',
and has interpreted it as 'wan' or 'bloodlessly white', a whiteness of
face that comes through unhappiness. Of course, this *may* be its
sense in the original poem also.

It is worth mentioning that the more natural translation of the
first word would be 'green', not 'blue', though Pound was probably
not aware of this. I would surmise that it was partly the oddity of
the grass being called 'blue' that attracted Pound to the poem.
'Blue' strikes a 'Chinoiserie' note – for one thing, because willow-
pattern plates are blue. On the other hand, it is the only exotic note
in Pound's poem; thus it is a good example of his careful
controlling of the dose of exoticism and 'oriental' oddity. It is not
just a matter of Chinoiserie however; for 'blue' is obviously
appropriate in English to melancholy – we feel 'blue', we sing
'Blues', we combat 'the blue devils'. It is probably also relevant that
an American would be more familiar with the idea of 'blue grass',
since it is a common type of pasture in Kentucky.)

Here, finally, are two other translations of the poem.

> The roses on her cheek blush bright,
> Her rounded arm is dazzling white;
> A singing-girl in early life,

And now a careless roué's wife. . .
Ah, if he does not mind his own,
He'll find some day the bird has flown![6]

(H.A. Giles)

Green, green,
The grass by the river-bank,
Thick, thick,
The willow trees in the garden.
Sad, sad,
The lady in the tower.
White, white,
Sitting at the casement window.
Fair, fair,
Her red-powdered face.
Small, small,
She puts out her pale hand.
Once she was a dancing-house girl,
Now she is a wandering man's wife.
The wandering man went, but did not return.
It is hard alone to keep an empty bed.[7]

(Arthur Waley)

Arthur Waley was a distinguished expert on Chinese literature, and his translations have a considerable reputation. He was, however, fairly plainly influenced by *Cathay*, and I must say I find Pound's version much the finer. To take an example, Waley's repetitious 'Green, green', 'Thick, thick' have a monotonous and rather puddingy effect, whereas Pound's repetitions are most poignant. (The Giles version is not a very serious competitor! I have included it for fun, and because it is through this version that Pound would first have got to know the poem.)

5. Homage to Sextus Propertius

In the year after the publication of *Cathay* (1915), Pound at last felt
equipped to undertake a large-scale work, and he embarked on *The
Cantos*. The work was to be an epic of sorts – but very much 'of
sorts', for, unlike the *Iliad* or the *Odyssey* or *Paradise Lost*, it was
not to have a plot in the ordinary sense. Moreover its heroes were
not to be warriors or demigods but artists and philosophers – or
rather not them so much as the new art-forms and new ways of
feeling they had pioneered. It was to be an 'aesthete's' epic, you
might say. But, as I have mentioned, this first scheme was later to be
abandoned; and the critic George Dekker is probably right in
saying that these early *Cantos* represented not much more than 'an
American literary tourist rambling genially round things that are
more pleasant to think about than current affairs and contemporary
landscapes'.[1]

While he was at work on his 'epic', however, Pound became
increasingly interested in the Latin elegiac poets, and, in a letter of
July 1916 to his friend Iris Barry, recommending a list of reading to
her, he said that if she found the existing versions of Catullus and
Propertius unsatisfactory he might have to 'rig up' translations
himself. His interest in these poets was coloured by a personal
comparison. For, in the years of Rome's growing imperial
greatness, they had written of love and private feelings – making a
cult of love as did their lineal successors the Provençal troubadours.
Here was something significant for Pound. For he was on the
threshold of his own 'epic', but an epic of a very inward and

actionless, not to say sedentary, kind, without the excitement of drums and trumpets; and the deliberate adhering to private themes by Catullus and Propertius became a support to him.)We remember how much his swashbuckling polemics were in defence of the right to be sensitive and to cultivate 'the algae and the tentacles of the soul'.[2] Also, this was Britain and 1916. Pound was living at the headquarters of an empire as great and overweening as the Roman, and that empire was now engaged in a war so hideous as to sicken one for ever of martial epics.

Thus, by very logical steps, Pound was led to the assumption of another major *persona*, that of the Roman poet, Sextus Propertius (c.50–16 BC). Propertius had published a book of elegies of which the theme was the joys and torments of his love affair with a courtesan, whom he calls Cynthia. In this he was continuing the tradition of the Greek elegists (in particular the Alexandrian poets Philetas and Callimachus) of the third century BC; and for a Roman poet this was, in its way, an act of defiance, or so Propertius pretended.(A right-thinking Roman poet would write about arms and the public weal, not 'effeminate' sexual intrigue.)Thus an ironic defensiveness runs through Propertius's elegies. Some are born for the battlefield, or to celebrate the battlefield, he says; others, less heroic in their fate, are destined for the narrower, though no less bitterly-contested, battlefield of the bed. He complains to fate for making him one of these latter; but at the same time he foresees a day when lovers will revere the tomb of this veteran of the wars of the bedchamber.

Propertius's first book of elegies won him a reputation, and he was drawn into the circle of Maecenas, the famous patron of Virgil and Horace; and it is implied in his succeeding elegies that Maecenas and others urged him to abandon love poetry and celebrate the imperial exploits of Augustus. Perhaps indeed they did so seriously, and Propertius's position began to be like that of a writer in Soviet Russia; more likely it was just a fiction cultivated by Propertius for his own purposes. At all events certain of his succeeding poems exhibit his serio-comic efforts – doomed to failure – to imitate Homer and his own contemporary, Virgil, and to celebrate martial exploits and patriotic mythology.

Here, in Sextus Propertius, so Pound felt was a 'mask' beautifully adapted to his own face; and during the third year of the war he embarked on the series of free translations and imitations which became *Homage to Sextus Propertius*. As he said of the poem later:

it presents certain emotions as vital to me in 1917 faced with the
infinite and ineffable imbecility of the British Empire, as they were to
Propertius some centuries earlier when faced with the infinite and
ineffable imbecility of the Roman Empire.[3]

The fact that, to respond to such a giant event as the 1914–18 war,
Pound needed to adopt a mask, or resort to obliqueness at all, may
seem strange: it was certainly the exact opposite of Wilfred Owen's
reaction. However, one should remember that, to poets of the past,
it is Owen's magnificent 'speaking out' that would seem the more
strange and the greater novelty.

A further attraction for Pound in Propertius was the fact that
he felt he had 'got through' to Propertius the poet better than the
professional scholars had done. (It was a feeling he was prone to.)
Propertius, as Pound saw him, was a subtle and original ironist – a
poet reminiscent of the French *Symboliste* writer, Jules Laforgue.
The field in which he thought Laforgue, and Propertius before him,
excelled was what he termed *logopoeia.* Pound, in 'How to Read',
distinguished three aspects of verse, as follows:

> *Melopoeia,* wherein the words are charged, over and above their
> plain meaning, with some musical property, which directs the
> bearing or trend of the meaning.
> *Phanopoeia,* which is a casting of images upon the visual imagination.
> *Logopoeia,* 'the dance of the intellect among words', that is to say, it
> employs words not only for their direct meaning, but it takes count
> in a special way of habits of usage, of the context we *expect* to find
> with the word, its usual concomitants, of its known acceptances, and
> of ironical play. It holds the aesthetic content which is peculiarly the
> domain of verbal manifestation, and cannot possibly be contained in
> plastic or in music.[4]

Pound's definition of *logopoeia* is not altogether clear, but from
other references it appears that what he meant was the playing off
of one kind of diction against another for ironic effect. Evidently
the diction of a Shakespeare tragedy will be different from the
diction of a *New Statesman* review or an Iris Murdoch novel and
the reader accepts each diction as the natural one for that kind of
writing. The employer of *logopoeia* undermines this unquestioned
acceptance by sliding disconcertingly from one kind of diction, with
its particular associations, to another. He, as it were, puts the
'diction' of his poem in inverted commas, reminding the reader that
all such dictions are arbitrary conventions.

Will you now read section 1 of *Homage to Sextus Propertius*
(*Selected Poems*, pp.79–81)? You will notice at once the effect
Pound seems to have in mind in his account of *logopoeia*, a

continual shifting of tone and style. See if you can pick out specific
words and lines responsible for such shifts.

DISCUSSION

In the first few lines, the tone is formal and staid, sounding like
some old-fashioned translator; in the next few lines ('Who hath
taught you so subtle a measure. . .') a subtle singing or dancing
measure creeps in. Then we have what is plainly not so much
translation as a paraphrase with commentary ('Out-weariers of
Apollo will, as we know, continue their Martian generalities. . .'),
followed by a snapping piece of wit ('We have kept our erasers in
order'), which, we can make a good guess, is pure Pound and
corresponds to nothing in the original. With 'A young Muse with
young loves clustered about her. . .' the style grows elevated and a
fraction over-inflated, and then with 'Annalists will continue to
record Roman reputations. . .' we are back with satirical paraphrase;
whilst with 'But for something to read in normal circumstances?'
we reach the tone of everyday conversation. And finally, those last
lines: they are rather noble and reverberative, surely – a fine
'straight' translation, though done in the concise and elliptical style
that we expect from Pound.

Pound, plainly is playing a variety of games in his translation.
Indeed, we should not think of it as a translation: the word we want
is 'imitation'. He is, in the first place, mixing classical allusions and
modern references: 'groves' and 'chariots' with 'erasers' and
'frigidaire patents'. He is also, it seems, deliberately leaving in
phrases here and there that remind us that this *is* a translation. Thus
the wording of

> Nor the monumental effigies of Mausolus,
> are a complete education of death

has the kind of stiffness one associates with Victorian translations
from the classics.

Then, what does one make of the following?

> Though my house is not propped up by Taenarian columns from
> Laconia (associated with Neptune and Cerberus)

Pound even seems to be 'taking off' notes to editions of the classics;
or perhaps a Baedeker.

Another kind of phrase puzzles us, too; for instance, in line 9,
'mellowed your whistles'. It faintly reminds one of 'wetting your
whistle' (facetious for 'having a drink'), and by contagion one

wonders whether one of the kinds of 'hall' mentioned two lines before might not have been a music hall. I would guess that for Pound this comes under the heading of *logopoeia*; he is not only using words for their direct meaning but also taking into account, in a special way, of habits of usage, of the context we *expect* to find the words in. 'Pamphlets' (line 64) might be another case. In modern English a volume of poems would not be called a 'pamphlet', though it is one of the words that would be given in a Latin-English dictionary to translate Propertius's word 'libellus': 'pamphlet' now suggests a scholarly article or polemical tract, written in prose. The word is deliberately wrong; Pound is not just making fun of incompetent translators, he deliberately means to remind us of the different literary and publishing conditions of the ancient world. Or again, take 'orgies' (line 4). He has translated Propertius's 'orgia' or 'mysteries' by its literal equivalent in English, thus again confronting the ancient world with the modern, which has lost its recollection of the religious nature of orgies. (We saw him doing the same sort of thing with 'mouth-organ' in *Cathay*: see pp.39.)

We shall come across all these things again in the succeeding sections, but I suggest that, as a way of getting the hang of Pound's 'Propertius' manner, you should study the first section fairly thoroughly. I will supply a few notes on allusions:

Line

10	*Apollo* was the god of poetry.
	Martian generalities means, presumably, platitudes about war and feats of arms. Mars was the god of war.
20	*forked hill* Parnassus, a mountain sacred to the Muses, had two peaks, one of which was sacred to poetry. (To anyone brought up on the classics, this is a very trite allusion.)
27	*deal-wood horse* The Trojan horse. Deal is a name for cheap wood.
29–32	*Achilles, etc.* These are all figures in Homer's *Iliad*.
32	*Ilion* was the citadel of Troy; 'Troia', which Pound mangles into 'Troad', was the town and the area round it.
33	*Oetian gods* Hercules died on Mount Oeta; but Pound was probably not aiming at much more than a 'classical-sounding' name.
42	*Orpheus* He performed these feats by playing on his lute.
43	*Citharaon* The legend actually was that Amphion played his harp so skilfully that the stones left the mountain,

> *Cathaeron,* and arranged themselves in the form of city walls. Pound, deliberately or otherwise, has muddled the story.
>
> 46–47 *Polyphemus* was a Cyclops who fell in love with the sea-nymph, Galatea.

As you will see, Pound's classical allusions tend to fall into two categories: very commonplace ones, which the general reader has a good chance of knowing; and ones that we could hardly be expected to understand, because he has muddled them. If his allusions seem daunting, this should reassure us. The truth is, Pound was not at all a deep classical scholar; he was by professional standards fairly ignorant and – this is the interesting point – pretended to be even more ignorant than he was. There has been considerable controversy about the 'howlers' in his *Homage to Sextus Propertius,* which still infuriate some scholars. I shall come back to this, but the point to take hold of here is that Pound is, in a sense, on the side of the ignorant reader. If one loves the poets of one's own language, and incorporates them into one's life without necessarily treating them as things to 'study', it is only natural to want to get to know foreign or classical (or for that matter ancient Chinese) poets in the same spirit. And part of the theory behind Pound's eccentric approach to translation is that this *can* be done – more easily than scholars tend to suggest.

Will you read Section II now?

As an exercise, trace out the variations and transitions in tone in the section in the way that I did for part of Section I.

Will you now re-read the rest of *Homage to Sextus Propertius* once or twice? Its sections run as follows: *I–II* Propertius declares his poetic vocation, which is to be a love elegist not a writer of patriotic epics. *III* He receives a summons from Cynthia. *IV* He questions his slave Lygdamus about Cynthia's frame of mind. *V* He returns to the subject of *I–II.* *VI* He contemplates death. *VII* He commemorates a night of love. *VIII* Cynthia is ill, and he imagines her dying and causing jealousies among the gods. *IX* He prays for her recovery. *X* Love and drink impel him to Cynthia's house in the early hours of the morning. *XI* He complains that there is no escape from love. *XII* a *reprise* of various earlier themes, in the course of which he makes fun of his rival Virgil's *Aeneid,* the patriotic poem *par excellence.*

Let us have a look at Section VI. To begin with, what is the sequence of thought in the opening seven lines?

> When, when, and whenever death closes our eyelids,

Moving naked over Acheron
Upon the one raft, victor and conquered together,
Marius and Jugurtha together,
                              one tangle of shadows.
Caesar plots against India,
Tigris and Euphrates shall, from now on, flow at his bidding . . .
                                        Selected Poems (pp.81–8)

Propertius imagines the day of death. (He is thinking of his own
death, but, as 'our' suggests, perhaps that of Cynthia too, or of all
men.) The next moment we are presented with a vision of the 'great
ones' of the earth being ferried to the underworld: pathetic, naked,
and on a raft – the most 'naked' of conveyances. The tone is
solemn, imaginative and compassionate, and without irony (save
for the irony of fate implied in victor and vanquished sharing the
same raft). Then, with 'Caesar plots against India' we are, with the
familiar Propertius/Pound irony, witnessing one of the great ones of
the earth in his hour of (somewhat futile) greatness.

There is something odd in this sequence of thought; indeed the
logic of these opening lines is all wrong by conventional standards.
What is the link between Propertius's death and that of the great
generals, Marius and Jugurtha?[5] It is not stated. And then, one
might have expected to hear of Caesar's hour of greatness before
being told of the fate that lies in store for greatness.

But if wrong by conventional standards, it is surely wonderfully
right by poetic standards – and especially the standards of
'modernist' poetry? For this is not a didactic poem, describing the
'greatness' of Caesar and then drawing the tombstone moral 'Death
comes to all alike'. It is not in the form of an argument, that is to
say; it is more a matter of setting two contrasting feelings side by
side. We are meant to hear those impressive lines, 'Moving naked
over Acheron. . .' (echoed a little later by 'One raft on the veiled
flood of Acheron') as a chord of deeper feeling sounding simultane-
ously with the ironic Propertian speaking-voice. And this is a model
of how the whole poem works, and of how many 'modernist'
poems work (Eliot's in particular). Subtler, or at any rate novel,
effects can be achieved by simply juxtaposing passages in contrasting
tones instead of relating them by argument as, say, Shakespeare or
Milton might have done in a sonnet, or as Gray does in his *Elegy in
a Country Churchyard*.

Then one asks oneself what Pound, or Propertius, is saying
about death in this poem? What attitude to death is he recommending? It seems to be that the exploits of generals and emperors,
whatever good they may do for their nation, leave the doers
themselves with nothing enduring. They go naked to the underworld;

whereas the poet at least takes with him his own books, which even death cannot destroy. But this said, let us not make too great a fuss about death, for neither pompous funeral ceremonies nor overdone mourning will be wise or in good taste. Death is a staggering fact, but one must retain an aplomb in the face even of death.

Thus that aplomb, or pose of imperturbability, that we saw Pound exploring in those epigrams in *Lustra* shows itself here a stronger more resourceful affair than we realized; it is more than social sophistication, it is an attitude fit to outbrave death itself. (It is interesting that Pound was quite shocked when Eliot, once, confessed to him that he was afraid of death.[6])

There is much more to comment on in this section. For instance that insistent, tripping tune, constructed out of repetition, which we first hear in the opening line:

When, when, and whenever death closes our eyelids

and which returns at

Enough, enough and in plenty

and again in

In vain, Cynthia. Vain call to unanswering shadows,

It is, one feels, almost a gay tune, certainly not a funereal one; and it contributes its quota to the complex poise or aplomb with which the poem confronts death.

Let us now look at Section VII (*Selected Poems*, pp.89–90). What do you make of the first two words? Of the second line? What kind of English is this? And what is its effect? Reading through the Section, do you notice a marked change of tone, and can you account for it?

DISCUSSION

'Me happy': it looks like pidgin English, doesn't it? It is, at any rate, as I think one may guess without knowing any Latin, a close take-off of a Latin construction. As we noticed before, Pound travels the whole length of the spectrum from the freest possible paraphrase of Propertius to the most comically literal rendering.

Do you agree with me that 'Oh couch made happy by my long delectations' is a wonderfully funny line? If so, I think the reason may partly lie in its context. The immediate joke in the line is the value Pound extracts from the Latinate primness of 'delectations', but he has prepared for this effect. The first line, 'Me happy, night. . .' is not really English at all but imitation Latin. By the

second line we are approaching normal English but, as 'delectations'
remind us, we have not yet quite reached it.

A very witty opening, then. But by the third part of the section,
'While our fates twine together. . .', an earnest eloquence enters.
The poem slows down; there begin to be long expressive pauses,
emphasized by the way Pound has laid out the poem on the page.
We pause very lengthily and meditatively between

> For long night comes upon you
>   and a day when no day returns.

The movement changes again at 'Fool who would set a term to
love's madness', and it goes through many further changes and
modulations. Musical organization has taken over in the later part
of the section, and what has begun as a witty, worldly poem has, by
natural progression, become a rapt, mysteriously beautiful hymn to
sexual love. One need no doubt – for all the feeling of the verse
confirms it – that this devout emotion is genuine and serious in
Pound.

So far I have shirked the question of how much it would help
us with Pound's poem if we knew Propertius's original. Pound
would have claimed that his poem stood on its own feet; and this
would not conflict with his claim to have 'seen' Propertius more
clearly than the scholars. Sometimes he denied that the poem was in
any sense a translation – though this was partly, no doubt, because
he was sore at attacks on his scholarship. Can we, then, forget or
ignore Propertius? The answer is not too easy. For one thing Pound
makes us very curious about Propertius, and there would be
something stupid in stifling this curiosity. Again, the way Pound
has rearranged his materials is sometimes rather striking. I will give
an example. Section VI is actually made up out of three separate
poems by Propertius. The first line and all that follows from 'Nor at
my funeral' are from a poem in which Propertius imagines his own
death. The 'Moving naked over Acheron' passages comes from
another poem, in which Propertius praises peace, as the god of
lovers, and condemns war. And the 'Caesar plots against India'
passage is based on a third poem in which Propertius gives
Augustus Caesar patriotic encouragement (though saying that it
will be enough for himself if he can witness Caesar's triumph like
any humble spectator in the street). What Pound has done with his
material strikes me as an inspiration of genius.

Then, a passage like the one in Section I, where Propertius
dutifully cites the mythological parallels of Orpheus and 'Citharaon'
and Galatea, promising himself – with a plunge into bathos – 'We

must look into the matter', gains an added humour if you know Propertius's tendency to long and tedious mythological catalogues. This was a besetting vice of Latin authors, and Pound may be right in implying, as he does here, that Propertius thought it ridiculous himself; still, he practised it, and Pound is here tweaking Propertius.

Equally, some of Pound's mistranslations are exceedingly witty. The Latin reads, literally: 'You (i.e. Virgil) produce such a poem as the Cynthian god modulates with his fingers upon his skilful tortoiseshell lyre'. To Pound, 'tortoiseshell' suggests 'tortoise', 'skilful' suggests 'trained', 'Cynthian' suggests 'Cynthia', and 'modulates' suggests 'tone down' or 'reduce my verse to your level'. Thus we get:

> Like a trained and performing tortoise,
> I would make verse in your fashion. . .
> (Section XII, lines 59–60)

> *Selected Poems*, p.97

Plainly, some of the joke of this is lost if one does not know the Latin.

And then, if one does know the Latin, one finds places where Pound seems to have muddled Propertius's sense to no good purpose.

> Orgies of vintages, an earthen image of Silenus
> Strengthened with rushes, Tegaean Pan,
> The small birds of the Cytherean mother,
>   their Punic faces dyed in the Gorgon's lake;
> (*Selected Poems*. p.82)

is a rather baffling version of something quite straightforward in the original:

> the mystic instruments of the Muses and the clay image of father
> Silenus, and thy reeds, O Pan of Tegea; and doves, birds of my lady
> Venus, the birds I love, dipped their red bills in the Gorgon's fount.

Again, by insisting, as he did, on mis-spelling names, e.g. writing 'Polydmantus' for 'Polydamas' (Polydamas was a figure in the *Iliad*; there is no such person as Polydmantus) he causes what appears to be quite useless confusion.

What used most to enrage classical scholars, however, and in some cases still does, is Pound's 'howlers'. I have mentioned one or two, and there is another notorious one in 'night dogs' (Section II, line 50). The Latin reads, literally: 'For thou shalt sing of garlanded lovers watching before another's threshold, and the tokens of drunken flight through the dark'. However, the word for 'thou shalt sing' – *canes* – happens to be spelt the same as the word for 'dogs'. Hence Pound's 'night dogs'! This is as rich a schoolboy howler as you could ask for. And was it a howler on Pound's part? Hostile scholars and critics gleefully say 'Yes'. Devoted defenders of Pound say 'No, quite absurd'. Here I would suggest the devoted defenders are in the right. Surely Pound is sometimes doing in this poem what I have described him as doing elsewhere (see p.20) – i.e. gazing at a page of foreign words with half-closed eyes till a sense, which may not be strictly the 'right' sense, swims out of it. Thus he is deliberately exposing himself to the risk of 'howlers'. So whether he was conscious of having made this, or any other, particular howler is hardly significant.

A point that strikes me as more interesting is that Pound's classical 'howlers' are, perhaps, indirectly a part of his critique of imperialism. For the classics had a special and symbolic prestige in Victorian and Edwardian Britain, as being the backbone of public school education and the training thought necessary, for some reason, for imperial administrators. (And whereas this use of the classics as a training-ground may have produced good Anglo-Indian magistrates and colonial governors, it did not do much for the classics – I mean, for intelligent appreciation of them as literature.) Thus Pound's classical howlers were a subtler and more judicious form of irreverence to the Empire than spitting at the flag.

I shall assume, then, that some readers of this book may want to explore Pound's original, the *Elegies of Propertius* – possibly for a variety of reasons – whilst othes, quite reasonably, will not. And for the sake of the former, here are the necessary references. The Book and poem numbers refer to the edition in the Loeb Classical Library series which has a prose version on the facing page.

Section no. in Pound	Based upon Propertius	Section no. in Pound	Based upon Propertius
I	Book III, nos. 1 and 2	VII	Book II, no. 15
II	III, no. 3	VIII	II, no.28B
III	III, no. 16	IX, 1	II, no.28B
IV	III, no. 6	IX,2,3	II, no.28C
V,1	II, no. 10	X	II, no.29A,B
V,2	II, no. 1	XI,1	II, no.15
V,3	II, no. 1	XI, 2	II, nos 30A and 32
VI	II, no. 13,	XII	II, no.34
	III, nos 4 and 5		

(Ronald Musker's translation, in the edition in the Everyman University Library series, is recommended if you wish to read a good modern version.)

6. Hugh Selwyn Mauberley

Somewhere about the end of the 1914–18 war and (we may surmise) after the writing of *Homage to Sextus Propertius*, Pound felt once again the wish to steer English verse in a new direction; and it appears that Eliot shared his feelings. Here is Pound's account, in the *Criterion* of July 1932:

> [Mr Eliot] displayed great tact, or enjoyed good fortune, in arriving in London at a particular date with a formed style of his own. He also participated in a movement to which no name has ever been given. That is to say, at a particular date in a particular room, two authors, neither engaged in picking the other's pockets, decided that the dilutation of *vers libre*, Amygism, Lee Masterism, general floppiness had gone too far and that some counter-current must be set going. Parallel situation centuries ago in China. Remedy prescribed *Emaux et Camées* or the Bay State Hymn Book. Rhyme and regular strophes. Result: Poems in Mr Eliot's *second* volume, not contained in his first ('Prufrock', *Egoist*, 1917), also 'H.S. Mauberley'.[1]

A few allusions need explaining here. 'Amygism' was Pound's rude nickname for the activities of Amy Lowell, the American poet who took charge of the Imagist movement after he defected from it (or perhaps her taking charge was why he defected – see p.12). Lee Masters was another American poet of the free-verse school, author of *Spoon River Anthology* (1916): Pound took a brief interest in him. More important, *Emaux et Camées* ('Enamels and Cameos') (1852) is a collection of poems by Théophile Gautier, who, having been an ardent Romantic as a writer, subdued his Romanticism in this volume to a more concise, witty and ironic style. He was also the originator, or at least the namer, of the 'Art for Art's sake'

movement, which claimed that art need and should have no
concern with social and political issues or indeed with anything
outside itself.

Almost all the poems in *Emaux et Camées* are in a tightly-knit
four-line stanza, and, as Ezra Pound implied in his retrospective
comment in *Criterion*, Gautier's verse-style influenced him a good
deal in *Hugh Selwyn Mauberley* (1920), the work that he produced
as a corrective to 'Amygism' and 'general floppiness'. It influenced
Eliot more directly. For instance in 'Whispers of Immortality' the
stanza

> Grishkin is nice: her Russian eye
> Is underlined for emphasis;
> Uncorseted, her friendly bust
> Gives promise of pneumatic bliss.[2]

is a direct echo of the first stanza of Gautier's 'Carmen'

> Carmen est maigre – un trait de bistre
> Cerne son oeil de gitana.
> Ses cheveux sont d'un noir sinistre,
> Sa peau, le diable la tanna.[3]

> [Carmen is lean – a sooty ring
> Circles her gypsy-like eye.
> Her hair is of a sinister black
> Her skin has been tanned by the devil.]

Gautier's influence on Pound extended beyond verse forms,
however, for *Hugh Selwyn Mauberley* is a poem about the rights
and wrongs of the 'Art for Art's sake' attitude, of which Gautier
was the earliest spokesman.

Would you now read the whole of *Hugh Selwyn Mauberley*
(*Selected Poems*, pp.98–112) once or twice? Don't worry if here
and there you find it a little baffling. (It is by no means all baffling,
or even difficult.) You may, though, be puzzled about the relation
between the two different parts of the poems: Sections I–XII with
the 'Envoi'; and the last five poems headed 'Mauberley 1920'.
If so, you will not be the first, for this is one of the main disputes
about the poem (and it has raised many disputes). Evidently there is
a relationship, for the first three poems of the 'Mauberley' second
part actually quote from the first part. Also, the very first poem of
all is entitled 'E.P. Ode pour l'Election de son Sépulchre', and while
E.P. must clearly stand for Ezra Pound, the whole poem is entitled
with the name of a fictitious character, Hugh Selwyn Mauberley.
So, part of the problem in relating the two parts must lie in deciding

the relationship of E.P. to Hugh Selwyn Mauberley. We will discuss this question later. Meanwhile, as you read through the poem, you should look out for its varieties of style. Try briefly to describe them. You should recognize some for their resemblance to earlier work by Pound we have looked at. But is there also an entirely new style? Consider, for example, the opening poem of the series. How would you describe it, and how does it differ from other styles in the poem? And, then, more broadly, what do you think the poem is about? What is its main theme or subject?

DISCUSSION

We will come to the point about style shortly, but I hope you agree that a broad answer to the question 'what is the poem about?' must be 'the rights and wrongs of the "Art for the sake of Art" point of view.'? In this it has a connection with *Homage to Sextus Propertius*, for to put the private before the public, as did Pound's Propertius, is not so very distant from putting Art before Life, especially since Propertius was a poet, and Pound's version of his poem celebrates poetic, before any other kind of achievement. Thus, in *Hugh Selwyn Mauberley*, we can say that Pound is not just reflecting on this general issue of Art for Art's sake, but also assessing his poetic career up to this time. (As I have said, Pound does return again and again to the theme of his own role, as a poet in society.) Let us run quickly through the various sections of the first part of the poem.

Section I, as we can gather from its title, is some sort of mock-epitaph on Ezra Pound himself. (The French title is an allusion to an ode by Pierre de Ronsard (1524–85), 'De l'élection de son sépulchre', i.e. 'The choosing of his tomb'.) We shall have to ask ourselves who is supposed to be composing this epitaph, and in what spirit, but its general drift is plain: his obituarist is describing him as a failure.

Sections II and III follow on from Section I in that they explain Ezra Pound's 'failure', in terms of a general decay of literary culture. Section II deals with the decay in Pound's own time, and Section III puts this decay into a larger historical perspective.

The theme of Sections IV and V is clear. Pound is evoking the 1914–18 war, setting its appalling human waste against the poorness of the civilization for which it was supposedly fought.

What about Section VI ('Yeux Glauques') to Section X ('Beneath the sagging roof. . .')? They must presumably be portraits of typical figures of the London cultural scene as Pound would have encountered them. We note that each portrait hints at or diagnoses some kind of failure.

Finally there is 'Envoi (1919)', a poem with an Elizabethan or seventeenth-century ring to it. I shall come back to this poem later.

DISCUSSION

Some features of the structure of the first part of the poem we shall leave for a moment, and consider what initial effect the poem has on us. You must have noticed at once that it combines poems in a number of different styles; and that is in fact how 'modernist' poets felt that a long poem had to be written. There are satiric portrait sketches, in tone not unlike those ironic epigrams we saw Pound writing earlier (pp.30–31); there is a very bold and original use of free verse in Sections IV and V; in 'Envoi (1919)' there is a pastiche of seventeenth-century English song-writing; and then, perhaps most striking of all, there is the style of the opening section 'For three years, out of key with his time. . .'. This last is a wholly new style for Pound. His comment of 1932 about the need to learn from Gautier (see p.55) is a help in defining the quality of this style for, for one thing, the style certainly could not be accused of 'floppiness'. It is a strenuously disciplined poetry, achieving great feats of concentration and condensation – a very *pregnant* poetry. Also it is, to a high degree, a poetry of the intelligence, written for a reader who will welcome wide-ranging allusions and a witty 'play of mind'. The reader has to make great leaps of thought and feeling at short notice.

Consider that stanza:

> His true Penelope was Flaubert
> He fished by obstinate isles;
> Observed the elegance of Circe's hair
> Rather than the mottoes on sun-dials.

Selected Poems, p.98

It surely concentrates an extraordinary amount of thought and imaginative suggestion into small compass? Of course, one needs to understand the allusions; but they are not very difficult allusions. Penelope was the wife whom, in Homer's *Odyssey*, Ulysses left alone in Ithaca while he went to fight against Troy. During his long absence she was beset by suitors, and she declared that she would make a choice of one of them when she had completed the piece of tapestry she was working on – tricking them, however, by unpicking at night what she had woven by day. Circe was the enchantress on whose isle Ulysses lingered for a whole year during his return from Troy. Flaubert, the French novelist (1821–80), was a supreme example of the devoted artist, labouring for hours and days to perfect a sentence.

We can thus roughly paraphrase as follows:

His true Penelope was Flaubert. His inspiration was the faithful and devoted artist Flaubert, who, like Penelope was forever writing and then rewriting his prose.

He fished by obstinate isles. He plied his art in the British Isles, which, as always, obstinately turn a deaf ear to serious art. But also, he practised a difficult art, one that dealt with recalcitrant and 'obstinate' artistic problems.

Observed the elegance of Circe's hair etc. He spent his time upon 'aesthetic' pursuits, as if time were no object (i.e. ignoring the mottoes on sundials about how time flies).

Notice, by the way, that this packed and pregnant style has particular appropriateness for two reasons. This is an epitaph, or mock-epitaph, on E.P., and one expects a condensed or 'lapidary' style on a tombstone. And secondly, the art of these very lines is a 'difficult' art, like that of their subject E.P. and E.P.'s model, Flaubert.

One observes, too, how, despite the tightly-knit verse form, Pound manages, when he needs to, to speak perfectly naturally, with the rhythm and emphasis of ordinary conversation:

> . . .Wrong from the start —
> No, hardly, but seeing he had been born
> In a half-savage country, out of date;
>
> *Selected Poems,* p.98

This playing off of freedom against restrictions is impressive, surely? Neither when he is speaking from behind a mask, as in 'Cino', nor when he attempts to be quite 'open', as in 'Commission', does Pound give us quite this sense of a man compelling verse to express his whole mind.

Let us now work through some of the later sections of Part 1, mainly just to ask ourselves what they are about. 'Yeux Glauques', for instance, must plainly be about the pre-Raphaelite movement. The woman with the 'faun-like head' is a survivor of the days of Rossetti and Burne-Jones and Swinburne. She has, or once had, the style of beauty, languid, vacant-eyed, half sensual, half spiritual, which was beloved of pre-Raphaelite painters; also, it seems, she was once a model for them. She feels out of place in Edwardian London, where her love-life, which in her youth scandalized the respectable, now seems to stir no one's interest. The poem also records how the 'English Rubaiyat' came to nothing. By this Pound must mean the Pre-Raphaelites' attempt to promote a pagan, Epicurean, un-Puritanical attitude to life and art, as expressed in that favourite book of Rossetti and his friends, Edward Fitzgerald's translation of the Persian *Rubaiyat of Omar Khayyam.*

You may not recognize all the references in the poem, e.g. 'Foetid Buchanan' and 'Cophetua' – and (on pp.69–73) I have provided some notes, explaining these and other allusions. But the general drift is clear.

What about 'Siena mi fe'; disfecemi Maremma'?

Equally plainly, this must be about a survivor of the 'Nineties, the period of Wilde and Dowson and Lionel Johnson, the period of 'decadence', *The Yellow Book* and the Rhymers' Club. It was a movement brought to a premature end by Oscar Wilde's trial and imprisonment, and there would have been many survivors with anecdotes to tell, in Pound's time and later.

In 'Mr Nixon', Pound is moving forward in time. This is the kind of successful commercial, or commercially-minded, writer fostered by the new publishing styles introduced in the 1890s: mass-produced cheap fiction, mass-circulation newspapers and periodicals, 'syndicated' columns etc. Actually Mr Nixon was probably based on Arnold Bennett.

There is a shade more difficulty in naming precisely what Pound is evoking in Section X, 'Beneath the sagging roof. . .', but a little reflection will remind us, at least, that the convention of artists and writers retiring to country cottages and the 'simple life' belongs, as a fashion, to the twentieth century rather than earlier. There are many reasons for this, ranging from the disappearance of an English 'peasantry' to the spread of tinned food. In fact it is a very interesting matter for sociological speculation. But perhaps all we need to do here is reassure ourselves that Pound is, once more, accurately evoking an aspect of the contemporary English cultural scene. (One cannot quite picture George Eliot or Matthew Arnold in a labourer's cottage on the South Downs.)

Section XII, ' "Daphne with her thighs in bark. . ." ' is pretty obviously akin to the section we have just been discussing, and depicts a fashionable literary hostess; but the opening stanza may puzzle you. Indeed, it puzzles most readers, and critics interpret it differently. So here we come up against one of the genuine kinds of difficulty in Pound's poem. I do not count allusions among these, because on the whole one can look allusions up. For instance the allusion in 'Daphne with her thighs in bark' is easily explained by a glance at a dictionary of classical mythology: Daphne was a nymph who, when pursued by Apollo, prayed for rescue to the gods, who transformed her into a laurel tree; also, which is relevant, Apollo was god of poetry. (Why the line should be in quotation marks is not so easily explained, and to save time here I will refer you to p.71; however, most of Pound's purpose is gained if you merely take in the fact that it *is* a quotation, ingeniously given a new meaning.)

We still need to ask, what is the *point* of the allusion, though. What is the resemblance between Daphne and Apollo, and a poet in a fashionable drawing-room? Does laurel – or do laurels – have any special association for us?

It must be that some sort of flirtation is involved between the Lady Valentine (the name faintly recalls Lady Ottoline Morell, of Bloomsbury fame) and the poet. One could read it like this: feeling herself protected by her expensive drawing-room, like Daphne protected by her foliage, the Lady Valentine reverses the myth and ever so discreetly *invites* 'Apollo's' advances: though whether what she is inviting him to do is engage in kisses or just cultural talk is uncertain – uncertain even to the poet. Anyway, the poem goes on to explain the nature of her interest in him: it is not much to do with poetry; it is more a kind of acquisitiveness or social insurance. Literature might be useful to her, for purposes of one-upmanship or as a political investment against some future revolution. (Poets are well-known to be 'bolshies'.) An additional possible implication in the lines is that the Lady Valentine, with her 'leafy hands', is offering the poet a laurel wreath i.e. crowning him as an immortal poet. To test this interpretation we have to ponder the first word of the third line: 'Subjectively'. (The way we are brought up short by that 'Subjectively', as we turn the corner of the preceding line-ending, exhibits Pound's *Mauberley* style in all its originality. It is a style that works by shock tactics and lightning-quick shifts of perspective.)

Those who take the lines to refer to crowning a poet with laurel would interpret the sense of 'Subjectively' as being that the poet, poor devil, has to do the crowning for himself. (He has to pretend to himself that the approval of this somewhat pretentious culture-snob represents 'success'.)

Perhaps the crowning-with-laurel idea is present, but I am inclined to regard the main meaning of 'Subjectively' as merely a stressing of the unreality of the Lady Valentine's interest in poetry and the poet's wry recognition that he, and the poetry he represents, is out of place in her drawing room. (And if it is out of place there, it is, as the poem goes on to say, equally out of place in Fleet Street, which in the day of Dr Johnson was the home of poetry but is now a market for haberdashery, literal or metaphorical.) It is perhaps only a matter of emphasis.

I am ignoring 'Brenbaum' and Section XI (' "Conservatrix of Milésien". . .'), for which see p.71, and come now to 'Envoi (1919)'. As with most of Part 1 there is no difficulty in enjoying this section as a poem in its own right, as I think you will agree. If you came across it in an anthology you might easily take it at first sight for an Elizabethan or seventeenth-century lyric. It is based on the famous poem 'Go, lovely Rose' by Edmund Waller (1606–87), which was set to music by Waller's contemporary Henry Lawes (1596–1662); and I think one might say that in its 'singing' quality, its flowing, winding, long-sustained, melodious line, which seems to be crying out for musical setting, it is not inferior to Waller. Here at any rate is Waller's poem for comparison.

Go, lovely rose

    Go, lovely Rose –
Tell her that wastes her time and me,
    That now she knows,
When I resemble her to thee,
How sweet and fair she seems to be.

    Tell her that's young,
And shuns to have her graces spied,
    That hadst thou sprung
In deserts where no men abide,
Thou must have uncommended died.

    Small is the worth
Of beauty from the light retired;
    Bid her come forth,
Suffer herself to be desired,
And not blush so to be admired.

    Then die – that she
The common fate of all things rare
    May read in thee;
How small a part of time they share
That are so wondrous sweet and fair!

I would draw your attention to something very beautiful in Pound's poem: I mean the halt and change of rhythm in the very last line, a change to a more tripping and dance-like movement, interrupting the smooth legato flow and forcing us into more attention to the actual sense – to good purpose, for what the last line says turns the poem into something one could regard as more serious than

Waller's: a defence of art as the sole permanent and indestructible human achievement.

Pound leaves us to guess what the section is doing here at this point of the poem, for 'modernist' poetry does not *explain*. However, if you consider that *Hugh Selwyn Mauberley* is about a 'failed' poet and about the decay of cultural traditions, this – surely rather fine, and certainly traditional – poem must provoke certain reflections. The poet seems to be saying, defiantly, that he is *not* such a failure after all, nor is poetry so much in decay, if he can compose so beautiful a poem in an ancient tradition.

But then, what is 'Envoi' actually saying? When one looks into it, it is not as simple as what Waller is saying. Nor is it clear beyond doubt who the 'thou' is in the third line – is it the lady or the book? According to which you decide, 'subjects' in the next line will mean either those paying homage to a ruler; or 'topics', the subject matter of a book or poem. And one might ask, too, whether the same lady is being addressed in all three stanzas. One critic, Donald Davie, argues that she is not a woman at all but England![4] Pound, when his biographer Charles Norman asked him in 1959: 'Who sang you once that song of Lawes?', was less than helpful; he answered: 'Your question is the kind of damn fool enquiry into what is nobody's damn business.'[5] It is an interesting question, what the 'Envoi' is actually saying; and my own view is that Pound is addressing three imaginary kinds of women, in his three stanzas. But there are more pressing questions to decide upon. And one of these cannot be shirked any longer; it is 'What is the relationship of Part 2 to Part 1?' This is more or less the same as asking 'What is the relationship of Hugh Selwyn Mauberley to Ezra Pound?'

Part 2 of *Hugh Selwyn Mauberley*

The first poem of Part 2 is certainly difficult. However, it seems that the poet (whether Hugh Selwyn Mauberley or Ezra Pound) was an artist who chose to practise a severely restricted and 'aesthetic' art, which left out most of the warmth and richness of life. The second section is equally difficult, but it clearly elaborates the same theme. The poet's 'fundamental passion' was not to deal with the large issues of life but to concentrate on small-scale formal problems, like an engraver of medallions. His poems are to be a series of 'curious heads in medallion' – something akin to Gautier's *Emaux et Camées*.

We then reach the third section, which relates, or enacts, the collapse that overtakes this poet. I say 'enacts', because we actually see it taking place, as if this were a psychological novel. The description of the collapse begins in the fifth stanza ('The coral isle ...'), and runs perhaps something like this: though wishing to concentrate on his exquisite, highly-disciplined, impersonal art, the poet finds his mind, against his will, filling with disturbing exotic daydreams. Life and nature are having their revenge on him, and before long he is incapable of highly-wrought art at all: all he is fit for is formless confessional outpourings – the very poetry most condemned by Ezra Pound and his school.

Section IV then takes us into his daydreams, the exotic, South Sea Island daydreams of the 'failed' poet; and at the conclusion of this section he composes his own epitaph.

My bald summary, inadequate all along, breaks down entirely here, for it leaves all the important questions unanswered. For instance, who is writing Section IV, Hugh Selwyn Mauberley or Ezra Pound? For it is, to my mind, a magnificent poem, intensely imaginative and, if you like, 'Romantic', yet wonderfully precise in its effects. Think of 'Washed in the cobalt of oblivion': what is being talked about is the hazy romantic blueness of distances, but the way it is expressed – with that specific and technical word 'cobalt' – reminds us that the poet talking to us is far from being the self-indulgent type of Romantic. The poet who writes this poem has not given in to daydreaming. Yet it is a very warm poem, not puritanically *condemning* exotic daydreams as you might have expected from the preceding poem. It appears that Ezra Pound must have some sympathy with the poet who decides to give up poetry and become a hedonist and pleasure-lover.

As for the final section, 'Medallion', the title, seemingly, provides a clue to its function in the poem. Presumably this is one of the poems, the 'curious heads in medallion', that the poet whose story we have been following composed before his breakdown? (It would thus be a sample of Mauberley's work, as 'Envoi (1919)' is a sample of E.P.'s?) Many things suggest this. For instance, 'Luini in porcelain!'[6] remains one of those lines in Part 2, 'The Age Demanded', describing Mauberley and his Art for Art's sake-ism:

> The glow of porcelain
> Brought no reforming sense
> To his perception
> Of the social inconsequence ... etc.

Selected Poems, p. 109

And the minute attention to facial detail in this concluding poem recalls the lines, in Part 2, Section II:

> This urge to convey the relation
> Of eye-lid and cheek-bone
> By verbal manifestation;

Selected Poems, p. 108

Above all, the poem reads as we should have expected it to: it is very 'aesthetic', very cold and exquisitely 'finished'. (It is a good poem, though, isn't it?)

It is a very curious thing to have done, this appending a second part to the poem, quoting from and commenting on the first, with a careful insistence upon chronology ('For *three* years'; 'Envoi (1919)'; 'Mauberley (1920)'), and if Hugh Selwyn Mauberley is a different person from E.P., then presumably, in some sense, Part 1 is E.P.'s poem and Part 2 is Mauberley's.

In *New Bearings in English Poetry* (1932), F.R. Leavis has some pages on the poem, which are in some ways the most sympathetic, and perhaps the best account of the poem there has been. However Leavis does not discuss the Pound v. Mauberley puzzle at all; and this should serve as a reminder that puzzles are one thing and poems are another and that we may get too absorbed in puzzles.

The Mauberley Puzzle

J.J. Espey, who has written a book about the poem, *Ezra Pound's 'Mauberley': A Study in Composition*, is predominantly interested in the puzzle, and he argues that Mauberley is at all points distinct from, and indeed the opposite of, Pound: he is 'precious' where Pound is robust, he is a sexual failure or eunuch who fails to realize when passion is offered him, and this lies at the root of his failure as an artist: his 'Medallion' is an example of sterile 'Art for Art's sake' poetry, all metallic 'surface' and contrasted altogether unfavourably with Pound's 'Envoi'. Espey supports his argument very ingeniously, suggesting for instance that, in Mauberley's 'new found orchid', Pound is making a ribald joke on two sense of 'orchid', a word which in Greek means 'testicle'. (The joke is symbolical of Mauberley's failure to respond to the sexual side of life.)

Donald Davie likewise, in his chapter on Pound in the *Pelican Guide to English Literature*, carefully distinguishes Mauberley from Pound. He says:

> Only now, with Part 2, does Mauberley, the titular hero of the whole work, emerge for our scrutiny, his emergence signalized by a new cross-heading 'Mauberley (1920)'. As with Eliot's Prufrock, so with Mauberley, the inability to come to grips with the world for the sake of art is symbolized in the ability to meet the sexual challenge, to 'force the moment to its crisis'. Mauberley, like (apparently)

Prufrock, allows the moment of choice to drift by without recognizing it, and is left with

... mandate
Of Eros, a retrospect.[7]

However, in 1965, in his book *Ezra Pound: Poet as Sculptor* Davie does a complete turnaround and argues that the poem has no real cohesion at all:

> In *Hugh Selwyn Mauberley* we look in vain for the developing 'plot' that commentators of all persuasions (including the present writer) have thought they found. Such 'plots' can indeed be found – all too many of them. The trouble is that any one of them requires that we give Pound the benefit of every doubt, on the score of elusive shifts of tone, a raised eyebrow here, a half-smile somewhere else, a momentary puckering of the brow. 'Tone' will not do so much, so certainly, as the most admiring commentators ask us to believe. Therefore, the two sequences are much more loosely jointed than they seem to be. Hardly anything is lost, and much is gained, if the poems are read one at a time, as so many poems by Pound, and if the *Mauberley* persona is dismissed as a distracting nuisance. *Hugh Selwyn Mauberley* thus falls to pieces, though the pieces are brilliant, intelligent always, and sometimes moving (for Gautier repeatedly enabled Pound to surpass himself). As for the theory of the persona, which served Yeats so well, it seems only to have confused Pound and led him to confuse his readers.[8]

This is rather shaking, especially from a critic who so recently held very different views. And if I cling to the feeling that there is such a poem as *Hugh Selwyn Mauberley* and that it is more than the sum of its parts, this is not because I think there is any 'plot' that will magic away all difficulties. (Actually I have my own 'plot', which you will find on p.73.)

What I feel is more important is to argue with Espey, for one needs to test a theory like his against one's emotional responses, and mine suggest to me that he is wrong. Pound's tone towards his aesthete is friendly and fraternal rather than hostile: that, at least, is how my ear is struck by the stanzas

The glow of porcelain
Brought no reforming sense
To his perception
Of the social inconsequence ... etc.

One can so easily imagine Pound himself, in another mood, adopting this 'Nineties'-ish pose of indifference towards public and social issues. Did he not do so in *Homage to Sextus Propertius*? And in the following section, 'Scattered Moluccas ...' he makes hedonism, the next stage in the aesthete's career, seem rather attractive in a way, or at least honourable. If the result of merely pleasing oneself is after a time to cease to exist altogether – well, there are worse fates; and the scene before the hedonist's dying eyes, an eternal South Sea idyll, is very seductive. Again, when in Stanza 12 of Part 2, 'The Age Demanded' Mauberley is condemned as a poet:

> Incapable of the least utterance or composition,
> Emendation, conservation of the 'better tradition',
> Refinement of medium, elimination of superfluities,
> August attraction or concentration.
>
> Nothing, in brief, but maudlin confession . . .
>
> *Selected Poems*, p. 110

the lines read better if one can feel an irony, a joke, in Mauberley being judged and condemned by what are notoriously Pound's own standards. And this irony will be that Mauberley is Pound himself, in one of his recurrent moods. 'There, but for the grace of God, go I' Pound is saying, with a friendly salute to one who, maybe, chose the wiser course after all.

Let me come back, finally, to the most important matter: how one is to enjoy Pound's poem. Consider those lines from Part 2, Section II:

> For three years, diabolus in the scale,
> He drank ambrosia . . .
>
> *Selected Poems*, p. 107

and especially the phrase 'diabolus in the scale'. It is a wonderfully suggestive phrase, isn't it? However, it was only when I came to write about Pound that I learnt what it actually refers to, <u>which is the augmented fourth in music</u> – <u>called 'the devil' or 'diabolus' by medieval musicians because it raised technical problems</u>. (The lines, by the way, are meant to remind us of the very first lines of *Hugh Selwyn Mauberley*:

> For three years, out of key with his time,
> He strove to resuscitate the dead art
> Of poetry . . .

which similarly employ a musical metaphor.) Hitherto I had vaguely thought of 'diabolus in the scale' as meaning something like 'taking the risk of hell and damnation' – i.e. 'For three years, with Art and the aesthetic life in one pan of the scales and the devil in the other'. I expect this reading was simply a mistake; yet it is not quite impossible that this was one of the half-formed secondary meanings in Pound's mind. At all events, one can guess that Pound welcomed that phrase 'diabolus in the scale' as 'right' in more ways than he originally intended. The phrase became poetry by creating a field of possible further meanings around itself. Pound who was master of the plain style, as in ' "Ione, Dead the Long Year" ', shows himself in *Hugh Selwyn Mauberley* as master also of an elaborate, extremely *verbal* manner. In lines such as these he is pinning his faith on happy accidents of language. One sometimes gets irritated with Pound for his high-handed way with allusions, but I do not feel it with the present poem. I had loved it and felt fascinated by it for twenty years before I understood half its allusions, and part of its charm must be that it *is* obscure, condensed and enigmatic, and meant to be. Pound himself once called *Hugh Selwyn Mauberley* a re-doing of *Homage to Sextus Propertius*.[9] But whereas in *Homage* he presents himself as relaxed, casual and insouciant, in *Hugh Selwyn Mauberley* he adopts almost the opposite pose: that of an austere diagnostician, determined to pronounce upon his age in the fewest and most highly-charged and highly-weighed words possible.

Leavis is undoubtedly right in regarding *Hugh Selwyn Mauberley* as a personal and deeply-felt poem (as he says, 'we feel a pressure of experience, an impulsion from deep within').[10] By this stage, I hope, some impression will have emerged as Pound as a man. I do not quite take Donald Davie's view that the theory of the persona only served to confuse him; but I think none the less that his interest in 'masks' and personae may point to an important fact – I mean, that he did not possess much self-knowledge or certainty about his own identity. As far as we have followed it, his career strikes me as inspiring: so much creativity, so much devotion to standards, so much practical generosity to other writers, surely demand admiration? Also, so far, it is a career full of comedy; for one cannot deny that Pound was a great show-off, and in a sense a great self-deluder, convinced that what he happened to know must be the be-all and end-all of knowledge. However, with hindsight, one may discern reasons why the career of such a man might later have dipped into tragedy.

Notes on some allusions in *Hugh Selwyn Mauberley*[11]

Epigraph The Latin words mean 'The heat calls [us] into the shade'.

Part 1

Section I

Capaneus One of the Seven against Thebes, struck down for defying the gods.

"Ἴδμεν γάρ τοι πάνθ' ὄσ' ἐνὶ Τροίη The Greek is from the Sirens' song in Homer's *Odyssey*: 'For we know all the toils that are in Troy'.

l'an trentuniesme etc. Adapted from the opening of *Le Grand Testament* by François Villon: the original reads 'En l'an trentiesme de mon eage' (in the thirtieth year of my age). Pound's French means 'In the thirty-first year of his age'. He originally wrote 'thirtieth', correcting it subsequently to 'thirty-first', the year in which he published the collection *Lustra*. Pound's poem, like Villon's, is a sort of 'last will and testament'.

Section III

mousseline of Cos In Roman times Cos was famous for the manufacture of thin and muslin-like clothing.

Sappho's barbitos The lyre, as associated with the famous Greek poetess Sappho (seventh century BC).

Dionysus The god of wine, standing here for the idea of 'pagan' freedom and acceptance of the body.

Heracleitus Greek philosopher (sixth century BC) who held that everything in the world was in a state of flux.

after Samothrace This seems to mean 'as did that of Samothrace'. Samothrace, an island in the Aegean, was an important centre for mystery cults. (There is a famous *Winged Victory* from Samothrace in the Louvre.)

τὸ καλόν Greek for 'the beautiful'.

Pisistratus A tyrant of Athens in the sixth century BC.

τίν' ἄνδρα, τίν ἤρωα, τινα θεόν, Adapted from Pindar (*Olympian Odes*, 11,2): 'What god, what hero, aye, and what man shall we loudly praise?'

Section IV

pro domo Latin: 'for the home'. Pound is alluding to, and varying, the well-known tag: 'Dulce et decorum est pro patria mori'. (It is sweet and fulfilling to die for one's fatherland.)

Section VI ('Yeux Glauques')

Yeux glauques French: meaning literally 'eyes of a bluish green'. 'Glauque' (in English 'glaucous') was very much a 'period' word of the 1880s and 1890s: absinthe was known as 'la sorcière glauque' (the green witch).

'King's Treasuries'   The opening chapter of Ruskin's *Sesame and Lilies* is entitled 'Of Kings' Treasuries'.

Foetid Buchanan   R.W. Buchanan published, under a pseudonym, a virulent attack on the pre-Raphaelite group, whom he referred to as the 'Fleshly School of Poetry', in *The Contemporary Review* in 1871.

cartons   i.e. cartoons.

Cophetua   An allusion to Burne-Jones painting *King Cophetua and the Beggar Maid*, now in the Tate Gallery.

maquero's   A maquero is a pimp; but Pound's meaning is, perhaps, closer to 'gigolo'.

Section VII ('Siena mi fe': disfecemi Maremma')

'Siena mi fe' etc.   Words spoken by La Pia in Dante's *Purgatorio*, V,134: 'Siena made me: Maremma unmade me'.

Verog   Monsieur Verog is based on Victor Plarr (1863–1929), a poet of the 1890s who became Librarian to the Royal College of Surgeons (and was thus aptly described as cataloguing 'pickled foetuses and bottled bones'; though Pound also means it metaphorically – i.e. that he is compiling a (faintly morbid) catalogue of relics and anecdotes of the Wilde era).

Galliffet   Alexandre Auguste de Galliffet (1830–1909), who led a brigade of *chasseurs* at the battle of Sedan in the Franco-Prussian war.

Dowson   Ernest Dowson (1867–1900), a 'Nineties poet.

Rhymers' Club   A club of poets founded about 1890 by W.B. Yeats and others.

Johnson   Lionel Johnson (1867–1902), another 'Nineties poet. He was a Catholic convert.

Headlam   Stewart Duckworth Headlam (1847–1924) was compelled by the Bishop of London to resign his curacy because he had lectured on theatre and dancing in a working-men's club. He founded the Church and Stage Guild with *Selwyn Image* (1849–1930).

'The Dorian Mood'   Victor Plarr published a book of verse entitled *In the Dorian Mood* (1896).

Section VIII (Brennbaum)

Pound seems to have drawn upon Max Beebohm, known as 'The Incomparable Max', for his Brennbaum, though Beerbohm was not in fact a Jew. The point of this section is not very clear, except that Brennbaum seems to represent the 'assimilated' Jew.

Section IX (Mr Nixon)

Dr Dundas A made-up name, perhaps representing some influential reviewer and 'bookman' such as Edmund Gosse or Edward Garnett.
friend of Blougram's The corrupt journalist Gigadibs in Browning's poem 'Bishop Blougram's Apology'.

Section X

The 'stylist' is possibly based on Ford Madox Ford (1873–1939), a friend and a novelist much admired by Pound.

Section XI

'Conservatrix of Milésien' One of Pound's most obscure allusions. It refers to a passage in Rémy de Gourmont's *Histoires magiques* (1894), in which Gourmont speaks of women who are 'preservers of Milesian traditions', i.e. who perform ancient sexual practices considered disreputable in the present day. The name 'Milesian' alludes to a famous Greek collection of erotic stories, the *Milesian Tales*, which has not survived. (This, somewhat contradicting what I say on p.58, is a case in which Pound is making absurd demands on the reader.)

Section XII

'Daphne' etc. A rendering of lines from Gautier's 'Le Château du souvenir':

> Daphne, les hanches dans l'écorce,
> Etend toujours ses doigts touffus . . .

Conduct etc. A rendering of two lines from Laforgue's 'Complainte des pianos qu'on entend dans les quartiers aisés':

> Menez l'âme que les Lettres ont bien nourrie,
> Les pianos, les pianos, dans les quartiers aisés.

'Conduct' here is a verb, not a noun.
Pierian roses Pieria was a place near Mount Olympus where the Muses were worshipped.

Part 2

Epigraph The Latin words, adapted from Ovid's *Metamorphoses*, vii, 786, mean 'bites at the empty air'.

Section I

Jacquemart   Jules Jacquemart was the engraver of the frontispiece to an edition of Gautier's *Emaux et Camées.*

Messalina   Wife of the Emperor Claudius, famed for her licentiousness.

Pier Francesca   The Italian painter Piero della Francesca (1416?– 92), one of the most austere and purest in style of Renaissance painters.

Pisanello   Vittore Pisanello (1397–1455), Veronese painter and designer of medals.

Achaia   Greece.

Section II

Epigraph   The French means: 'What do they know of love, and what can they know? If they don't understand poetry, if they don't respond to music, what can they understand of that passion in comparison with which roses are coarse and the scent of violets is a thunderclap?' 'Caid Ali' is Pound himself.

anangke   Greek for 'necessity'.

nuktis 'agalma   A Greek phrase from the poet Bion, meaning 'night's ornament'.

to agathon   Greek for 'the Good'.

wide-branded   Possibly a slip for 'wide-banded'.

irides   Irises. Pound, in this extremely obscure stanza, is possibly playing on the two senses of 'iris', i.e. the flower, as well as part of the eye.

botticellian   An allusion to the Italian painter Sandro Botticelli (1444–1510).

diastasis   A medical word, meaning 'separation of bones without fracture'. However, Pound seems to be using it in a sense of his own, compounded out of the Italian word 'disteso', or 'spread out', and 'dilation'.

     John J. Espey, in his *Ezra Pound's 'Mauberley'* (1955) has a complicated explanation of this stanza, drawing on the symbolism of Botticelli's painting *The Birth of Venus*. However, the basic meaning must presumably be something to the effect that Mauberley, being so intent on the aesthetic qualities of the female face, failed to notice its sexual invitation.

Orchid   Pound is possibly punning on the Greek meaning of the word 'orchid', i.e. 'testicle'.

Section III ('The Age Demanded')

red-beaked steeds of the Cytherean   The doves who draw Aphrodite's chariot. For their red beaks, see p.53.

Minoan undulation   Probably an allusion to the characteristic undulation of the lips of sculpted heads of the Minoan (early Cretan) period (i.e. another facial detail such as Mauberley was fascinated with).

apathein   Greek for 'impassibility'.

Section IV

Moluccas   Islands in the Malay archipeligo.

Section V (Medallion)

Anadyomene   Venus Anadyomene, or 'Venus Rising from the sea', as in Botticelli's *Birth of Venus*; though the particular representation of Venus that Pound refers to seems to be one by another artist, reproduced in Salomon Reinach's *Apollo* (1904), a book much studied by Pound.

My own small contribution to an interpretation of the poem's 'plot' is to suggest that the second part deals, not only with Mauberley's collapse, but – rather more explicitly than some critics imply – with a love affair, a *three-year* love affair. (Thus, for instance, 'the final estrangement' referred to in Section II, line 15 is an estrangement from a woman.) Mauberley muddled the actual love-affair through drifting and procrastination, and did not realize what he had missed till too late – though when it finally dawned on him, after much 'sifting' of his memories, it did so with earthquake-like force (see lines 16–19). He did, however, profit from it to the extent of being left with rich material for a poem. (I can't otherwise see what the 'three years' insisted on can refer to. It is too short for even a failed poet's career, but a plausible length for a love affair.)

7. Approaching *The Cantos*

The Cantos, whether one regards them as a masterpiece or a ruin, must be said to be Pound's *magnum opus*. However, it is not within the scope of this book to discuss them in detail. What I want to do, rather, is to suggest a frame of mind in which to approach them. First, let me insist on an important point: no one could understand or enjoy Ezra Pound's *Cantos* who was unfamiliar with the earlier Pound – the Pound of Imagism, of *Cathay* and *Propertius* and *Hugh Selwyn Mauberley*. His *Cantos* manner is the fruit of his experience and innovations in these earlier poems, and constantly reminds us of them. On the other hand, there is also much that is quite new in *The Cantos*, both in their design and in their texture. It is a poem that has puzzled and baffled many readers – as indeed it often puzzles and baffles me, about as often as it provokes my admiration, though it certainly does that too.

Pound had contemplated a poem of epic scale from quite early on but does not seem to have begun intensive work on *The Cantos* (it is significant that they never acquired any less non-committal title) until about 1915. One or two false starts ensued, and he published isolated portions (e.g. a 'Canto III' in the magazine *Poetry* in August 1917) which subsequently had to be scrapped or quite drastically revised. The poem seems originally to have been conceived in the form of a kind of soliloquy on the part of a Pound-like figure or surrogate, whose personality would provide the poem's ultimate focus – as it does in Browning's *Sordello*, which Pound greatly admired and in a certain sense was taking as a model. This scheme was then jettisoned in favour of a more impersonal form of presentation, or 'constatation', in the Imagist manner, and with it disappeared a verse-colloquy between Pound and Robert Browning about the appropriate form for a modern epic. (There is a relic of this passage at the beginning of Canto II: 'Hang it all, Robert Browning,/there can be but the one "Sordello".')

It seems plain that the poem was, from the start, conceived of as open-ended: that is to say, Pound had a wealth of material for it but not a detailed plan worked out in advance, indeed this would have been alien to his whole enterprise. That the poem as we have it does not correspond to some preliminary blueprint is plain, if for no other reason than that the Pisan Cantos (LXXIV–LXXXIV) deal explicitly with Pound's weeks as a prisoner in an American army detention camp near the end of the Second World War, an episode he plainly could not have foreseen in 1915. This fact in itself implies no deficiency in Pound's design. Form in art can be achieved retrospectively, as well as prospectively, and Pound was aiming at 'retrospective' form.

We are probably safe in assuming that from the start Pound saw his poem-to-be as an epic. This certainly is strongly suggested by its present opening, which insists on its kinship to Homer's *Odyssey.* That it should be the *Odyssey* rather than the *Iliad* that inspired Pound, i.e. the story of a hero who opportunistically adapts himself to (unforeseen) circumstances, rather than strives arrogantly to defy them like the protagonists of the *Iliad*, is a fact with bearing on the whole 'modernist' enterprise. (We remember that James Joyce was composing his *Ulysses* at the same moment; indeed it strongly influenced *The Cantos*.) Like any epic, *The Cantos* contain all kinds of material: myth, history and personal reminiscence; lyrical passages and doctrinal passages; dialogues, allegories, prayers and catalogues. On the other hand, unlike other epics, *The Cantos* will have no central plot or action; and this is a very big difference.

If one can imagine a man with the ability to isolate each of his innumerable experiences among people, books and works of art and to reduce it to its gist, so that it is for him recognizably *that* experience, not confusable with any other; and if you can also imagine that man setting all these experiences into meaningful relation; then you will have a vague idea of the kind of poet Pound aspired to be when composing *The Cantos*. And what you may also see is that, were he successful in his aim, he might be able to dispense with some of the props and crutches employed by traditional poets – even that most useful of all crutches, a plot. When one is baffled by a problem in life, one can always scrub the floor or tidy one's room, thereby giving oneself the sense of getting

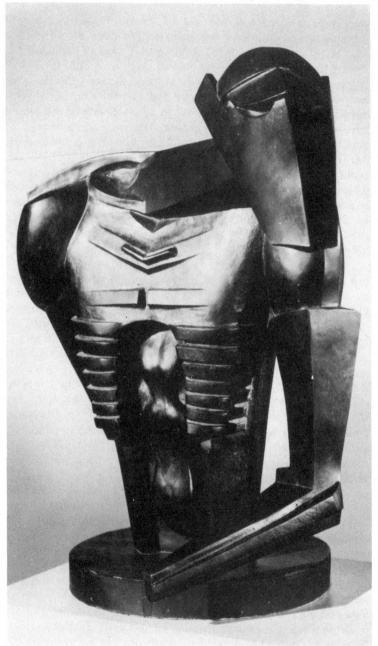

Rock Drill (1913–14) by Jacob Epstein (Tate Gallery)

something in order; and in a similar way, a writer of a long poem in the old style always had plenty of little practical tasks to be getting on with – planning the steps and details of his action, arranging symmetries between book and book or canto and canto, etc. These would be support to him in his job of setting his ideas in order in the deeper sense. However, one might feel – and it seems that Pound did feel – that if one's mind and experience were sufficiently in order, one could do without such supports and solaces. The loss would be enormous, but there might also be a gain. For an epic with a plot has, to some extent at least, to be read in one single direction. Whereas a plotless epic can be – as you might say – read backwards, forwards or sideways; its materials can develop interrelations more freely and multifariously than in a traditional epic.

Thus, in approaching *The Cantos*, one must not look for sequence, or a beginning, middle and end. The poem abounds in form, but form of a different kind. And one of the principles of its form is what Hugh Kenner, following Gerard Manley Hopkins, has well named as 'rhyme' – the rhyming, not of words, but of subjects, themes and incidents. '*The Cantos*', says Kenner, 'afford a thesaurus of subject-rhymes. Many heroes rhyme with Odysseus, and a house of good stone rhymes with mountain wheat, strong flour, the mind of Agostino di Duccio, and the proportions among the plain arches of St Hilaire in Poitiers'.[1] Here Pound was a great innovator, and the more one reads *The Cantos*, the more alert one's ear becomes to these 'subject-rhymes'.

A second fundamental point to grasp is that Pound's method is to begin by establishing what you might call his 'data'. 'The first cantos are preparation of the palette', Pound wrote to Felix Schelling on 9 July 1922. 'I *have to* get down all the colours or elements I want for the poem. Some perhaps too enigmatically and abbreviatedly. I hope, heaven help me, to bring them into some sort of design and architecture later.'[2] He establishes certain myths, such as the myth of Actaeon (see Canto IV); certain significant incidents, such as Cunizzo da Romano freeing her slaves (see Canto VI); or certain metaphysical conceptions, such as the conception of creative memory, as embodied in the *Canzone* 'Donna mi pregha' by the Tuscan poet Guido Cavalcanti (1250–1300) (see Pound's rendering of the poem in Canto XXXVI); and then, having done so, he can feel free to signal a reference back to these 'data', in later cantos, by means of a single phrase, or even a single word. Thus, for instance, the medieval Italian poet Cavalcanti's phrase '*dove sta memoria*' ('where memory liveth') recurs often in the *Pisan Cantos*

(LXXIV–LXXXIV), in a way that would mean nothing to a reader
who had not read Canto XXXIV. As the poem proceeds, Pound
depends more and more upon this kind of 'shorthand'; and, once
grasped, it is a perfectly comprehensible way of working, though I
know of no poet who attempted it before.

A third general point to remember is that Pound's approach to
history is not to talk *about* historical events or periods but to
present 'exhibits' – a sentence from a treaty, a letter or a part of a
letter, a disjointed snatch of conversation etc. This is confusing to
the reader, who sometimes feels like a visitor locked up for the
night in a museum – one of those mad provincial museums, where
Roman potsherds jostle Merovingian hairpins and the pellets from
owls' stomachs. However, the method follows logically from
Pound's whole approach to poetry and the world; it is simply an
extension of the fear of 'abstractions', that determination to stay
close to the 'concrete', which was the inspiration of Imagism.

This is a good point to mention another aspect of *The Cantos*:
Pound's bold innovations in the poetic use of typography. They
include great variability in indentation (i.e. the lateral placing
of verse-lines) and also in the spacing between lines; a wide variety
of fonts; and even variation in the weight of type. Pound had a
supremely sensitive ear, and the function of many of these
expressive devices is acoustic and relates to the subtleties of melody
and rhythm; others, however, are purely visual – though still
'rhythmic', for there is such a thing as visual rhythm. Somehow, the
look of the standard Faber edition of *The Cantos*, one of the most
beautiful books I know, confirms one's impression that these
typographic inventions are a work of genius, indispensable to his
own special purposes but of general utility as well. Other poets, for
instance T.S. Eliot and William Carlos Williams, seem to have felt
this and borrowed from them freely.

The question now arises, does the poem possess overall form?
Daniel Pearlman called this 'the crux of *Cantos* criticism': whether
'this physically enormous, sprawling poem has *major form* – an
overall design in which the parts are significantly related to the
whole'.[3] This in turn prompts Peter Brooker, in his helpful
Student's Guide to ask whether such a 'major form' is something
we actually have the right to demand. 'Criticism which shares this
assumption is limited to internal aesthetic and thematic questions in
The Cantos, and is locked, moreover – its differences notwith-
standing – in an organicist aesthetic which values formal unity to a
degree probably inappropriate to a poem which, like the Alps or the
ocean, has mass and boundaries but hardly coherence.'[4]

It would seem to me, though, that we ought to draw a distinction between 'unity' and 'coherence'. A thing (for instance, the seaweed of the Sargasso Sea) may be 'coherent', in the sense of being a mass of interconnections, without exactly constituting a 'unity'. I doubt if 'formal unity' is a quality that Pound's poem could ever have aspired to. It seems to imply some pattern that could, ultimately, be described rather simply; and whenever critics claim to detect some such simple design in *The Cantos* they sound, in my view, definitely unconvincing. I am not at all persuaded when Ronald Bush writes that: '*The Cantos* comprise an epic like the *Aeneid* or the [Divina] *Commedia*, which begins as the divine energies that are no longer harnessed by religious awareness sweep away an impious world. The poem proceeds through a hell of misdirected will, through a purgatorio where the old rituals are recaptured, to a paradise where "the shrine be again white with marble/. . . the stone eyes look again seaward".'[5] Such a pattern, among many other patterns, may be discoverable in *The Cantos*, if one digs for it, but this is quite a different matter from its constituting the poem's 'overall' design. The inferno/purgatorio/paradiso pattern in Dante's *Divina Commedia* – or, to take another example, the Odyssey pattern in James Joyce's *Ulysses* – works as a structuring device exactly because it is obvious.

The question of 'coherence' poses itself differently. That the question is relevant to Pound's ambitions seems plain, for in a very late Canto (CXVI), published three years before his death, he uses this word in what appears to be a confession of failure.

> I have brought the great ball of crystal;
> > who can lift it?
> Can you enter the great acorn of light?
> > But the beauty is not the madness
> Tho' my errors and wrecks lie about me.
> And I am not a demigod,
> > I cannot make it cohere.

> > > > > (*The Cantos*[6] pp. 795–6)

Let us not take that 'I cannot make it cohere' too literally – or rather, let it not make us jump to too quick conclusions. The point about Pound, it would seem to me, is not that he was careless about 'coherence' but on the contrary that he set peculiar store by it and believed, in his more optimistic moments, that he could bring off feats of coherence beyond the powers of other poets. Nor was it an unreasonable belief. To make such an odd collection of styles and themes as those in *Homage to Sextus Propertius* cohere (if you agree that they do) is an achievement most poets would envy; and in reading his free-form Imagist poems one is often reminded of his own favourite simile for a poem, and for the imaginative act generally, i.e. iron filings leaping into order at the approach of a magnet. The notion is put very eloquently in his *Guide to Kulchur*:

> The *forma*, the immortal *concetto*, the concept, the dynamic form which is like the rose pattern driven into the dead iron filings by the magnet, not by material contact with the magnet itself, but separate from the magnet. Cut off by the layer of glass, the dust and filings rise and spring into order. Thus the *forma*, the concept rises from death.[7]

The ordering force of Pound's imagination was very great: it would be no wonder, then, if he put too much trust in it and persuaded himself he had achieved coherence when he had not. It is my impression that to some extent this is what happened – a tragedy of *hubris*, if you like.

One needs to grasp that if the poem does not possess coherence on the smaller scale it cannot have it on the larger. Thus the true issue is not, I suggest, 'major' or overall form, but rather form within individual cantos and passages. I will give an example of what I mean. Will you read Canto II and then re-read lines 40–116? This passage draws on Ovid's *Metamorphoses* Book III, where it is told how Pentheus, King of Thebes, attempts to banish the new cult of Dionysus – the Roman Bacchus, also known as Lyaeus, god of wine and of inspiration and ecstasy – from his kingdom. He plans to arrest the young Dionysus, against the warnings of his grandfather Cadmus and the prophet Tiresias; and, in an effort to dissuade him, the mariner Acœtes tells him the story of what happened before, when an effort was made to kidnap Dionysus aboard a ship. Dionysus incited his train of lynxes to take over the ship and metamorphosed the ship into vines and creepers and the sailors (all but Acœtes, who took his side) into fish.

Pound's lines strike me as irresistible and quite magnificent. There is such vividness and concentration of language (as in 'void air taking pelt'); such masterly stylistic modulations, as when he evokes echoes of the Anglo-Saxon epics, 'northern' echoes, in this southern domain ('God sleight then, god-sleight:/Ship stock fast in sea-swirl'); such cleanness and precision in all the effects and such delicacy in the endless variations played on the same little rhythmic motif, a motif vaguely recalling the second half of a classical hexameter ('hot breath on my ankles', 'fur brushing my knee-skin'). Knowing Pound's Imagist style, moreover, the telescopings and condensations of sense strike us as familiar and do not cause us much difficulty, nor does the minor problem of knowing who is talking. (It is of course, the sailors at 'To Naxos? Yes, we'll take you to Naxos', Accœtes at 'And I said: "It's a straight ship" ', Dionysus (Lyaeus) at 'From now, Accœtes, my altars', and Accœtes again at 'And I worship./I have seen what I have seen.' The modern-life note in Accœtes' account of the pirate Lycabas or Lycabs ('an ex-convict out of Italy') is again a very mild example of Pound's *Propertius* manner.

It is a different matter, though, when one asks oneself how this passage hooks on to its context, and I have never seen this fully explained. That the whole Canto is in some sense about *meta-morphosis* is obvious enough and important. As we see, he has folded another metamorphosis, or anyway transformation, into the Dionysus one – that of the maiden Tyro wooed by the sea-god Poseidon, transformed into the river Enipeus. (Ovid, whose poem is an accumulation of legendary metamorphoses, might have asked, not being a 'modernist', what more we wanted in the way of form and coherence.) We tell ourselves, again, that Pound's obsession with translation, already a central preoccupation in *Cathay* and *Propertius* and even more prominent in the *Cantos*, could be equally called an obsession with metamorphosis. 'Metamorphisis' is a good name, or metaphor, for what he did to Propertius and to Chinese poetry; and Canto I presents a passage from Homer rendered via a Renaissance Latin translation into the style and diction of the Anglo-Saxon *Seafarer* – a strange succession of metamorphoses which, placed thus in the very opening Canto, is evidently meant to announce to the reader that 'translation' both in a narrow and a wide sense is going to be a leading preoccupation.) So the Canto is about 'metamorphosis'? Yes . . . but it is still not quite clear where this gets us. The word will be a prop to us, but it will not do to lean on it too heavily.

Still, this is only one possible linkage between the Dionysus passage and its context, and we shall expect in such a poem that there will be not just one but many links. Another is suggested by the long and beautiful invocation to the lynx, an animal sacred to Dionysus, in Canto LXXIX: and if this link is established, then the 'context' here is nothing less than the whole poem. Hugh Kenner has two more links to suggest. He writes of Canto II that 'The theme is the artist's struggle to bring form out of flux'. And he remarks, entertainingly, that 'Pound wrote this Canto about the time his countrymen were passing the 18th Amendment, outlawing the wine-god'.[8] (You will notice that Kenner cunningly avoids saying that Pound, when composing this vision of the danger of offending the god of wine, actually had Prohibition in mind.)

Still I am not satified. The sort of explanation that really counts with a poem, or any work of art, is the kind that makes a kind of 'click' in the mind, and none of the foregoing suggested links or explanations cause such click in my own mind, and if someone argued strongly to me that the Dionysus passage was *not* integrally linked to its context, I would not know how to confute him.

To put my point another way: 'explanations' such as critics provide are better thought of as 'descriptions', and as such they may have real value in the sense of helping us to see what is there in the poem. Descriptively at least, the following is helpful, as are many other *aperçus* scattered about Alexander's book and those of Hugh Kenner, Donald Davie and others.

> If *The Cantos* are not cast consistently in the form of a voyage of discovery, they are conducted in the spirit of such a venture, and continents or islands of knowledge, like Enlightenment America or Siena, or corners of Renaissance Italy, or China as seen via Confucianism, are explored and reported on. The amorous encounters of Odysseus with Calypso and Circe, and his interviews with other nymphs and goddesses, also serve as models for other realms of Pound's experience. The visit to Hell, initiated in Canto I, is resumed in *propria persona* in XIV and XV. Incidents from the *Odyssey* are specifically used as ways of dealing with actual experience – shipwreck, landfall, passing of Lotus-Eaters, the encounter with Proteus, the loss of companions.[9]

*   *   *

All that I have said so far forms a sort of precautionary preface. I shall go on to indicate a few landmarks in the poem; for, where a good deal is perplexing, anything that helps one get one's bearings is valuable. But what I do *not* want to suggest is that these landmarks constitute the framework or skeleton, the 'overall design', of the poem.

Canto I

Pound begins his poem by plunging us into a version of Book XI of Homer's *Odyssey*, where Ulysses, by means of a blood-sacrifice, raises the spirits of the dead. Pound's version, based on a Latin translation of Homer by the Renaissance poet Andrea Divus, is composed in an imitation of the style of the Anglo-Saxon 'Seafarer'. This complicated 'overlaying' of different cultures, ancient Greek, medieval, Renaissance and modern, gives a foretaste of similar overlayings in the poem as a whole. The reference to Ulysses (or

Odysseus) is important, for, through much of the poem, Ulysses's voyagings among the islands and along the indented coasts of the Mediterranean serve as a parallel to Pound's wanderings through cultural history. There is also some implication that, in his activities as a translator, he, like Ulysses in his sacrifice, is bringing the dead to life.

8-11

Cantos VIII–XI   Malatesta Cantos

These cantos present a picture of Sigismundo Malatesta (c.1417–68), Lord of Rimini and munificent patron of art and letters. He is chosen by Pound to represent <u>the creative or 'factive' personality.</u> His violent and bloody career ended in disaster, leading to excommunication and the expropriation of his possessions; but he left as his permanent memorial and imprint on history the magnificent Malatesta Temple at Rimini. The relation of active life to art symbolized by Malatesta is an important thread in Pound's poem.

14-15

Cantos XIV–XV   Inferno

This is Pound's hell or inferno, comparable with the infernal scenes in the *Aeneid*, the *Divine Comedy* and *Paradise Lost*. It is, as Eliot remarked, <u>'a hell for other people'</u>, containing all Pound's *bêtes noires*: usurers, 'perverters of language', etc.

20

Canto XX (line 110 onwards)   Lotus-Eaters

In the *Odyssey*, Ulysses and his companions come to an island inhabited by people who live on the fruit of the lotus, which induces joyous oblivion and destroys all desire to return to one's native country. (Cf. Tennyson's poem 'The Lotus-eaters'.) Pound, in these very fine lines, seems to identify the lotus-eaters with the Hugh Selwyn Mauberley type of aesthete, and the passage throws light on the poem *Hugh Selwyn Mauberley*.

24-26

Cantos XXIV–XXVI

This is <u>an evocation of the maturity and decline of Venice.</u>

31-34

Cantos XXXI–XXXIV   Jefferson

Deals with the political ideas and actions of Thomas Jefferson, third president of the United States and a hero to Pound, who depicts him as another example of the 'factive' personality.

42-44

Cantos XLII–XLIV   Founding of the Monte dei Paschi

Pound takes the story of the founding of the bank known as the Monte dei Paschi, in Siena, under the auspices of Cosimo, first Duke of Tuscany, as an example of socially beneficial and non-usurious banking.

45

Canto XLV   'Usura' Canto

An eloquent 'complaint' against usury, in medieval verse-style. There is a reprise of it in Canto LI. *51*

Canto XLIX   49

A Chinese-style lyric poem, celebrating the rhythm of agricultural labour and of the seasons. Hugh Kenner calls this beautiful section 'the emotional still-point of the Cantos'.[10]

52-59

Cantos LII–LXI   Chinese History

A chronological progress through Chinese history to the death of the Manchu emperor Yong Tching in 1735, showing the wisdom of the ancient *Li Chi* or *Book of Rites*, as consolidated by Confucius, going into action history. To a considerable extent the text is a mosaic of quotations and half-quotations from the twelve-volume *Histoire générale de la Chine* (History of China) by J. de Mailla (Paris, 1777–83) and from the five Confucian classics: the *Book of Rites*, the *Analects*, *The Great Learning*, the *Doctrine of the Mean* and the *Book of Odes*.   禮記. 論語大學幅詩經

62-71

Cantos LXII–LXXI   American History   *Adams*

The chronological progress continues but the scene changes to America, where Confucian wisdom is traced in the actions of John Adams, one of the fathers of the American revolution, who was born in 1735. (A parallel is implied with Sigismundo Malatesta, see Cantos VIII–XI.) The text is a mosaic of fragments from the ten-volume *Works of John Adams*, ed. C.F. Adams (Boston, 1850–6).

74-84

Cantos LXXIV–LXXXIV   Pisan Cantos

Reflective cantos against a prison-camp background, in which Pound affirms the power and fruitfulness of 'creative memory'. Pound here speaks somewhat more in *propria persona* than hitherto in the poem, and his mind ranges freely over the 'data' established earlier in *The Cantos*.

85~95

Cantos LXXXV–XCV   Section: Rock-Drill

The title refers to Jacob Epstein's sculpture *Rock Drill* (see p. 000). Pound saw an early plaster version of this sculpture in Epstein's studio in 1913, in which the man was bestriding a real pneumatic drill. (There is an analogy perhaps to the 'real' documents or exhibits inserted by Pound into *The Cantos*.) Michael Alexander writes: 'This section is called *Rock-Drill* because Pound . . . is drilling a way to the *Thrones of Paradise*, through public incomprehension and his own despair'.[11]

96-109

Cantos XCVI–CIX   Thrones

Pound said in an interview: 'The thrones in Dante's *Paradiso* are for the spirits of the people who have been responsible for good government. The thrones in the Cantos are an attempt to move out from egoism and to establish some definition of an order possible or at any rate conceivable on earth'.[12]

110~117

Cantos CX–CXVII   Drafts and Fragments

*   *   *

52 – 071

It will be seen that Cantos LII to LXXI stand in contrast to the remainder of the poem in presenting a linear progress through time – ten Cantos of Chinese history, and ten of American history in the shape of one man's career (that of John Adams, the second President of the USA). Pound's method of narration is, admittedly, not exactly 'linear', being a curious and often bewildering 'mosaic' method, entailing here and there some jumbling of temporal order. Still, for the purposes of these two symmetrical decads of Cantos, he largely abandons the feature so characteristic of the earliest Cantos and of some later ones: the dizzying cross-cutting between different cultures and epochs, likened by Michael Alexander to 'someone twiddling the tuning dial on a powerful radio receiver'.[13] This makes these two decads 'easier', in a certain sense. There seems fairly general agreement, however, that, at least in the case of the Adams Cantos, it also makes them less rewarding and interesting. Pound sometimes gives the impression in them of a man doggedly and joylessly completing a task that he has set himself.

Why he thought the task was necessary is a question that takes us to the heart of his political beliefs, and I will end with a brief comment on this tragic aspect of Pound. There is a certain idea tempting to a poet, and especially a 'modernist' poet such as Pound, so obsessed with artistic *discipline*: it is that the organizing of a nation resembles the organizing of a poem. It is, I think one must insist at once, a delusion and a dangerous delusion; nevertheless it is a surprisingly tempting one, and Pound is not the only poet who has been betrayed into it, though no other poet suffered such harm from it. What attracted him to Jefferson and John Adams and Mussolini was the thought that they were artists, 'artifexes', 'factive personalities' like himself: they did not merely direct or regulate the nations that they served but suffused them with their own creative energy. 'Treat him [Mussolini] as *artifex* and all the details fall into place', he wrote.[14] 'If you don't believe that Mussolini is driven by a vast and deep "concern", a will for the welfare of Italy, not Italy as a bureaucracy, or Italy as a state machinery stuck up on top of the people, but for Italy organic, composed of the last ploughman and the last girl in the olive-yards, then you will have a great deal of trouble about the un-Jeffersonian details of his surface.' Later in the same book he specifically compares governmental organization to poetic metre. 'My next analogy is very technical. The real life in regular verse is an irregular movement underlying. Jefferson thought the formal features of the American system would work, and they did work till the time of General Grant, but the condition of their working was that inside them there should be a *de facto* govenment composed of sincere men willing the national good.'[15]

The decisive step in Pound's political progress may perhaps be said to have been his introduction, *via* the Fenollosa papers, to Confucianism. For in Confucianism, regarded in a certain light, there seemed to be clear support for his dearest wish, which was to find an analogy – and more than analogy, an obscure identity – between the organization of a work of art and the organization of a nation. Did not Confucius not only serve as a Prime Minister, with signal success, so that young aspirants to government were sent to study under him, but also (according to tradition, anyway) classify the Odes (i.e. the corpus of classic Chinese poetry), arrange the national *Book of Rites and Ceremonies*, and set in order the music of temple and court – and with the implication that government, poetry, music and ritual were in a sense all aspects of one and the same thing? At the heart of Confucian teaching lies the notion of personal self-culture, as the *sine qua non* of effective government. '. . . the prince must have in himself not one but all of the qualities that he requires from others, and must himself be empty of what he does not want from others in reflex':[16] so runs Pound's own translation of the Confucian *Great Digest*, which he completed in the 1950s. Or again, 'one humane family can humanize a whole state; one courteous family can lift a whole state into courtesy; one grasping and perverse man can drive a nation to chaos. Such are the seeds of movement.'[17] If poetry is a form of self-culture, a refining of the faculties and discipline of the heart, then, according to a Confucian view of things, it has the closest possible affinity to the art of government.

This was plainly an intoxicating thought to Pound; it was indeed exactly what he most wanted to hear, and it is what underlies his cult of the 'factive intelligence', as represented by Sigismundo Malatesta, Jefferson, Adams, Mussolini and Confucius himself. No better key to the 'Chinese' Cantos (LII–LXXI) is required than the following, from Pound's own translation of *The Great Digest*:

NOTE
Starting at the bottom as market inspector, having risen to be Prime Minister, Confucius is more concerned with the necessities of government, and of governmental administration than any other philosopher. He had two thousand years of documented history behind him which he condensed so as to render it useful to men in high official position, not making a mere collection of anecdotes as did Herodotus.

His analysis of why the earlier great emperors had been able to govern greatly was so sound that every durable dynasty, since his time, has risen on a Confucian design and been initiated by a group of Confucians. China was tranquil when her rulers understood these few pages. When the principles here defined were neglected, dynasties waned and chaos ensued. The proponents of a world order will neglect at their peril the study of the only process that has repeatedly proved its efficiency as social coordinate.[18]

It could also be said that the problem of the 'American' Cantos (LXXII–LXXXI) *as poetry* is that Pound does not succeed in convincing us that his Confucian doctrine is right and that the new United States stand in relation to John Adams and the other founding fathers as a poem does to its author. Pound is not seeking to persuade us of this rhetorically but to prove it by a 'concrete' demonstration, and we (anyway I) do not get the feeling that it has been proved. His 'demonstration' turns out to be mere rhetoric after all.

I have stressed Pound's political beliefs rather than his economic ones because it is here that one can see more easily how Pound, for not at all disreputable reasons (for after all, an admiration for Confucius is no crime), could have been led into his monstrous views of the 1930s period. His economic theory, to put it at its very simplest (and it *was* pretty simple), was that <u>any healthy financial system needs to be based on the natural abundance of the earth, and that a 'usurious' system (like western capitalism) in which 'money breeds money' is inherently pernicious: it is sterile and 'against nature', and deserves to be bracketed (as it was by the medieval church) with sodomy, another 'sterile' activity, or with contraception.</u> (The lines in the 'usury' Canto XLV: 'It hath brought palsey to bed, lyeth/between the young bride and her bridegroom' must presumably refer to contraception?)

Now, I think this is a false doctrine, and Pound's effort to demonstrate it as a truth in *The Cantos* arouses a painful mixture of questions. One's reaction is partly grudging admiration, for there is no doubt he sincerely believed he had found a new way of dealing with such matters in verse – writing, for instance, to Mary Barnard on 13 August 1934[18]: 'I have, confound it, to forge pokers, to get economic good and evil into verbal manifestation, not abstract, but so that the monetary system is as concrete as fate and *not* an abstraction etc.'[19] One also feels a queer discomfort, at least I do, at the fact that, whereas I don't think Aquinas was right about usury or that Pope John Paul II is right about contraception, one finds Canto XLV entrancing. And lastly, one feels intense horror that Pound's economic theory should lead him to brutal vilification of Jews, as a people supposedly dedicated to 'usury'.

However, if Pound's economic theory is false, it is not so false as his basic political theory. Indeed it is perhaps not so much false as the perversion of an important truth, and one would know how to set about arguing against it and rebutting it. Whereas his political theory is such a leap of faith, that it is hard to see how one could ever demolish it by rational argument.

Our route here leads us round from Pound's political beliefs to Pound the poet. A question that must raise itself is why, with all his creative originality, Pound did not achieve more than he did. Part of the answer, I suggest, may be that, though he certainly had things to say in verse, he had nothing quite so important or urgent or profound to say as Eliot or Yeats. It is true that according to strict 'modernist' doctrine a poet, or at least a poem, should not have to 'say' anything: a poem should not 'say' but 'be'. However, I am not fully convinced by this doctrine. At least, it seems obvious to me that Yeats and Eliot, and Pound also, were passionately concerned to say something, to express beliefs in their verse – quite as much as Wordsworth or Shelley, and more so than Tennyson, though it was

Ezra Pound by Wyndham Lewis

said more obliquely. And when a poet is so concerned to 'say' something there comes a moment when we judge him or her by what is said. As far as Pound is concerned, all his deepest beliefs were bound up with aestheticism as a philosophy of life. Pound faced this fact courageously in *Hugh Selwyn Mauberley*. Nevertheless it is a constricting outlook, and it may be that his political madnesses sprang from a desperate effort to escape from its constrictions.

Notes and References

Chapter One (pp.1–10)

1   S. Hynes, *The Edwardian Turn of Mind* (London, OUP: 1968) p. 308.
2   C. Norman, *Ezra Pound* (London, Macdonald: 1960; 1969 edn) p. 245.
3   W.B. Yeats, *The Collected Poems of W.B. Yeats* (London, Macmillan: 1950) pp. 88–9.
4   H. Kenner, *The Poetry of Ezra Pound* (London, Faber: 1951) p. 301.
5   See J. Hone, *W.B. Yeats: 1865–1939*, 2nd. ed. (London, Macmillan: 1962) p. 272.
6   *The Dial*, Vol. 85, Jan–June, 1928, p. 5.
7   T.S. Eliot, *'The Waste Land': A Facsimile and Transcript of the Original Drafts, Including the Annotations of Ezra Pound* (London, Faber: 1974).
8   Pound's wartime broadcasts on behalf of the Fascists, a most repellent series of utterances, have been published in *'Ezra Pound Speaking': Radio Speeches of World War II*, (ed. L.W. Doob, 1978). See also: Ezra Pound, *Jefferson and/or Mussolini* (1935) p. 34.
9   See Hugh Kenner, *The Pound Era* (London, Faber: 1972) p. 556.

Chapter Two (pp. 11–17)

1   The phrase is F.S. Flint's in a brief 'History of Imagism', printed in *The Egoist*, II, 5 (1 May 1915). See John Press, *A Map of English Verse* (London, OUP: 1969) p. 44.
2   See 'A Retrospect' in *Literary Essays of Ezra Pound* (Ed. T.S. Eliot; London, Faber: 1954) p. 4.
3   See discussion of Vorticism on pp. 36.
4   As for Note 2, pp. 3–4.
5   'Vorticism' in *Fortnightly Review*, 1 September 1915, reprinted in Ezra Pound, *Gaudier-Brzeska: A Memoir* (London, Bodley Head: 1916) p. 98.

6   Latin: 'the scattered limbs of nymphs'.
7   T.S. Eliot, *Collected Poems 1909–1962* (London, Faber: 1963) p. 73
8   William Carlos Williams, *The Collected Early Poems of William Carlos Williams* (London, MacGibbon and Kee: 1938) p. 340.

Chapter Three (pp. 18–32)

1   'Psychology and the Troubadour', *The Quest*, vol. IV, no. 1, pp. 43–4.
2   T.S. Eliot, *To Criticize the Critic* (London, Faber: 1965) p. 185.
3   D. Davie, *Ezra Pound, Poet as Sculptor* (London, Routledge: 1965) p. 34.
4   H. Kenner, *The Pound Era* (London, Faber: 1972) p. 190.
5   'To break the pentameter, that was the first heave', Canto LXXXI, line 54.
6   W.B. Yeats, 'A General Introduction to my Work' in *Essays and Introductions* (London, Macmillan: 1961) p. 522.
7   Ezra Pound, *Gaudier-Brzeska, A Memoir* (London, Bodley Head: 1916) p. 98.
8   Ezra Pound, *The Spirit of Romance* (London, Dent: 1910) p. 190.
9   Walt Whitman, 'Song of the Open Road' (1856) in *Leaves of Grass* (1881).

Chapter Four (pp. 33–43)

1   Ernest Fenollosa, *The Chinese Written Character as a Medium for Poetry*, (Ed. Ezra Pound; San Francisco, City Light Books: 1936) pp. 12–13.
2   *Ibid.*, p. 29.
3   For an account of Vorticism, see p. 36.
4   H. Kenner, *The Pound Era* (London, Faber: 1972) p. 202.
5   T.S. Eliot, 'Introduction' to Ezra Pound, *Selected Poems* (Ed. T.S. Eliot; London, Faber: 1928) p. 14.
6   Translation by H.A. Giles *History of Chinese Literature* (London, Heinemann: 1901) p. 98.
7   Translation by Arthur Waley *170 Chinese Poems* (London, Constable: 1936) p. 40.

Chapter Five (pp. 44–54)

1   G. Dekker, *Sailing After Knowledge, The Cantos of Ezra Pound* (London, Routledge and Kegan Paul: 1965) p. 150.
2   'Commission', *Selected Poems*, p. 44.
3   D.D. Paige (Ed.) *The Selected Letters of Ezra Pound, 1907–1941* (London, Faber: 1950) p. 231.
4   Ezra Pound, *Literary Essays of Ezra Pound* (London, Faber: 1954) p. 25.
5   Gaius Marius (d. 86 BC) defeated and captured Jugurtha, King of Numidia, and brought him as a prisoner to Rome, where he was executed.
6   H. Kenner, *The Pound Era* (London, Faber: 1972) p. 336.

Chapter Six (pp. 55–73)

1   'Harold Monro', *Criterion*, Vol. XI, No. 45, July 1932, p. 590.
2   T.S. Eliot, *Collected Poems 1909–1962* (London, Faber: 1963) p. 55.
3   T. Gautier, *Emaux et Camées*, ed. A. Boschot (Paris, Garnier, n.d.) p. 93.
4   D. Davie, *Pound* (London, Fontana: 1975) p. 54.
5   C. Norman, *Ezra Pound* (London, Macdonald: 1960; 1969 edn) p. 224.
6   The painter, Bernardino Luini (c. 1475–1532) was a follower of Raphael.
7   D. Davie, in *Pelican Guide to English Literature, Vol. 7: The Modern Age* (London, Penguin: 1961) p. 327.
8   D. Davie, *Ezra Pound, Poet as Sculptor* (London, Routledge: 1965) pp. 100–1.
9   F. R. Leavis, *New Bearings in English Poetry* (London, Chatto and Windus: 1932) p. 138.
10 Based mainly on K.K. Ruthven, *A Guide to Ezra Pound's 'Personae'* (Berkeley; University of California Press: 1969).

Chapter Seven (pp. 74–90)

1   H. Kenner, *The Pound Era* (London, Faber: 1972) p. 93.
2   D.D. Paige (Ed.) *The Selected Letters of Ezra Pound, 1907–1941* (London, Faber: 1950) p. 180.
3   D. Pearlman, *The Barb of Time, On the Unity of Ezra Pound's Cantos* (New York, OUP: 1969) p. 3.
4   P. Brooker, *A Student's Guide to the Selected Poems of Ezra Pound* (London, Faber: 1979) p. 228.
5   R. Bush, *The Genesis of Ezra Pound's Cantos* (Princeton University Press: 1976) p. 266.
6   Quotations from *The Cantos* are from *The Cantos of Ezra Pound* (Revised collected edition (Cantos 1–117); London, Faber: 1975).
7   Ezra Pound, *Guide to Kulchur* (London, Faber: 1938; 1952 edn) p. 152.
8   H. Kenner, *The Pound Era* (London, Faber: 1972) p. 368.
9   M. Alexander, *The Poetic Achievement of Ezra Pound* (London, Faber: 1979) p. 124.
10 H. Kenner, *The Poetry of Ezra Pound* (London, Faber: 1951) p. 32.
11 M. Alexander, *op. cit.*, p. 212.
12 K. Dick (Selection) *Writers at Work: The* Paris Review *Interviews* (London, Penguin: 1972) p. 112.
13 M. Alexander, *op. cit.*, p. 152.
14 Ezra Pound, *Jefferson and/or Mussolini*(London, Stanley Nott: 1935) p. 34.
15 *Ibid.*, p. 95.
16 Confucius, *The Great Digest and Unwobbling Pivot*; translation and commentary by Ezra Pound (London, Peter Owen: n.d.) p. 61.
17 *Ibid.*, p. 59.
18 *Ibid.*, p. 19.
19 D.D. Paige (Ed.) *The Selected Letters of Ezra Pound, 1907–1941* (London, Faber: 1950) p. 260.

Further Reading

Works by Pound

Verse

The standard editions of the verse are as follows:
Collected Early Poems ed. M.J. King (Faber, 1977)
Collected Shorter Poems (2nd ed. Faber, 1968)
The Cantos of Ezra Pound (Faber, 1975)
Selected Poems, ed. T.S. Eliot (Faber, 1928). This has a valuable
    Introduction by Eliot.
Selected Cantos (Faber, 1967)
Selected Poems 1908–1959 (Faber, 1975). Quotations in the text are from
    this edition.

Translations

The Translations of Ezra Pound, ed. Hugh Kenner (Faber, 1953; rev. ed.
    1970)
The Classic Anthology Defined by Confucius (Faber, 1955)
Sophocles; Women of Trachis (Faber, 1956)
Certain Noble Plays of Japan (Cuala Press, Dundrum, 1916)
Ta Hio: The Great Learning. Newly rendered into the American Language
    by Ezra Pound (University of Washington Book Store, 1928)
Confucius: The Great Digest and the Unwobbling Pivot (Faber, 1952)

Prose

The Spirit of Romance (Dent, 1910; rev. ed. Peter Owen, 1953)
Gaudier-Brzeska: a Memoir (Bodley Head, 1916; new ed. Marvell Press,
    1960)
'*Noh' or Accomplishment*, by Ernest Fenellosa and Ezra Pound (Mac-
    millan, 1916; new ed. as *The Classic Noh Theatre of Japan*, New
    Directions, New York, 1959)
Pavannes and Divisions (Knopf, New York, 1918)
√ *Instigations*, including *The Chinese Written Character as a Medium for
    Poetry* (Faber, 1967)

ABC of Economics (Faber, 1933)
√*ABC of Reading* (Routledge, 1934)
Make it New (Faber, 1934)
Jefferson and/or Mussolini (Stanley Nott, 1935)
Polite Essays (Faber, 1937)
√ *Guide to Kulchur* (Faber, 1938)
The Letters of Ezra Pound, 1907–1941, ed. D.D. Paige (Faber, 1951)
√ *Pound/Joyce: the Letters of Ezra Pound to James Joyce with Pound's essays on Joyce*, ed. F. Read (Faber, 1968)
√ *Literary Essays of Ezra Pound*, ed. T.S. Eliot (Faber, 1954). This is a very extensive selection, containing a substantial proportion of Pound's best critical writing.
Selected Prose, 1909–1965, ed. W. Cookson (Faber, 1973)

Works about Pound

Biography

P. Hutchins: *Ezra Pound's Kensington. An Exploration 1885–1913* (Faber, 1965)
J. Cornell: *The Trial of Ezra Pound* (Faber, 1967)
Mary de Rachewiltz: *Discretions* (Faber, 1971) a memoir by Pound's daughter
C. Norman: *Ezra Pound* (Macdonald, 1960, rev. ed. 1969)
N. Stock: *The Life of Ezra Pound* (Routledge, 1970)

Criticism

General
√ H. Kenner: *The Poetry of Ezra Pound* (Faber, 1951). Strongly recommended. *The Pound Era* (Faber, 1972)
√ D. Davie: *Ezra Pound: Poet as Sculptor* (Routledge, 1965). Strongly recommended.
D. Davie: *Pound* (Fontana Modern Masters, 1975)
√ C. Brooke-Rose: *A ZBC of Ezra Pound* (Faber, 1971)
√ *New Approaches to Ezra Pound*, ed. Eva Hesse (Faber, 1969)
Ezra Pound: the Critical Heritage, ed. E. Homberger (Routledge, 1972). An extensive selection of critical comment.
Ezra Pound: a Critical Anthology, ed. J.P. Sullivan (Penguin Books, 1970) Ditto.
M.L. Rosenthal: *A Primer of Ezra Pound* (Macmillan, New York, 1960)
M. Alexander: *The Poetic Achievement of Ezra Pound* (Faber, 1979)
P. Brooker: *A Student's Guide to the Selected Poems of Ezra Pound* (Faber, 1979). A useful guide to allusions and bibliographical facts.
√ A. Durant: *Ezra Pound, Identity in Crisis* (Harvester Press, 1981). Applies Lacanian psychology to the reading of Pound.

Earlier Poems

N.C. de Nagy: *The Poetry of Ezra Pound. The Pre-Imagist Stage* (Francke Verlag, Berne, 1960)
T.H. Jackson: *The Early Poetry of Ezra Pound* (OUP, 1969)

K.K. Ruthven: *A Guide to Ezra Pound's Personae* (University of California Press, 1969)

Wai-Lim Yip: *Ezra Pound's Cathay* (Princeton University Press, 1969)

J.P. Sullivan: *Ezra Pound and Sextus Propertius: a Study in Creative Translation* (Faber, 1965)

J.J. Espey: *Ezra Pound's 'Mauberley': a Study in Composition* (Faber, 1955)

The Cantos

G. Dekker: *Sailing After Knowledge. The Cantos of Ezra Pound* (Routledge, 1963)

R. Bush: *The Genesis of Ezra Pound's Cantos* (Princeton University Press, 1976)

D.D. Pearlman: *The Barb of Time: On the Unity of Ezra Pound's Cantos* (Oxford University Press, New York, 1969)

N. Stock: *Reading the Cantos: a Study of Meaning in Ezra Pound* (Routledge, 1967)

Index